EXTRAORDINARY RESULTS FOR LIFE

Discover Your Path to Be UN-ordinary

JOHN,

SUCH A PLEASURE TO FINALLY MEET YOU — WISHING YOU NOTHING BUT EXTRAORDINARY SUCCESS

ALSO BY JOE CONTRERA

*LIGHT 'EM UP! How to Ignite the Fire
in Your Sales Team in Just 21 Days*

I Could Love No One…Until I Loved Me

*EXTRAORDINARY RESULTS FOR LIFE:
Discover Your Path to Be UN-ordinary*

*EXTRAORDINARY RESULTS: Mastering the Art
of Leading, Coaching, & Influencing Others*

EXTRAORDINARY RESULTS FOR LIFE

Discover Your Path to Be UN-ordinary

JOE CONTRERA

AWP

Copyright © 2022, Joe Contrera and ALIVE @ WORK® LLC

All rights reserved. The use of any part of this publication, reproduced, transmitted in any form or by any means, electronic, mechanical, photocopying, recording or otherwise stored in a retrieval system, without the prior consent of the publisher is an infringement of the copyright law.

ALIVE @ WORK® PUBLISHING
1–877–972–5483
www.aliveatwork.com

The Pro Book Editor, editor
David Moratto, cover design
IAPS.rocks, interior design
Tantillo Productions, audio engineer

LCCN: 2022906331

Issued in print, electronic, and audio format.

ISBN: 978-0-9747602-4-7 (hardcover)
ISBN: 978-0-9747602-5-4 (e-book)
ISBN: 978-0-9747602-6-1 (audio book)

This book is dedicated to my parents, Augustine (Gus) Contrera & Rosie "Bananas," the two people who had the single biggest influence on my life, in so many ways that I cannot count and in many ways I have yet to discover.

Some folks believe you choose your parents before you arrive here on Earth to learn the lessons you must learn. I couldn't have made a better choice!

TABLE OF CONTENTS

ALSO BY JOE CONTRERA ii
INTRODUCTION xiii
    The Path to an *UN*-Ordinary Journey Begins… xv
    A Process, Not a Destination xvi
PART I 1
    CHAPTER 1: THE CHALLENGE TO BE UN-ORDINARY 3
        Time To Wake Up 4
        What We Were Taught Instead 4
        Defining Extraordinary 5
        It's Your Business and It's Personal 6
        Still Want to Be Extraordinary? 8
    CHAPTER 2: THE WAKE-UP CALL 9
        The Alarm Goes Off – Time to Wake Up 10
        Who's Developmentally Challenged? 10
        Questions, Questions, and More Questions! 11
    CHAPTER 3: ARE YOU SURE YOU WANT TO WAKE UP? 13
        The Cost of Living Your Life Asleep 14
        Is Ignorance Really Bliss? 15
        Helicopters and Lawn Mowers 16
        Embracing Change 17
    CHAPTER 4: THE THEORY OF NON-CHANGEABILITY (INFLEXIBILITY) ... 19
        The Ego 20
        Your Ego 20
        My Supreme Court 22
        Egoic Theory and the Need to Be Right 22
        Egoic Theory and the Need to Be in Control 23
    CHAPTER 5: DIS-SOLVING THE EGO 25
        Your Ego Does Not Want to Be Dis-Solved 25

Life is Filled with Paradox	26
Reducing the Ego – Part I	27
Reducing the Ego – Part II	28
Humility	29
Humiliation	29

CHAPTER 6: THE 1ST LEVEL OF CHANGE – THE PUSH 31

In the Beginning	31
Seasons of Change	31
Looking Out the Picture Window of Life	32
Exercise: Reflection	33

CHAPTER 7: THE 2ND LEVEL OF CHANGE – THE PAIN 35

Change or Die and Let's Make a Deal	35
Temporary Quicksand	36
Pain as the Catalyst to Change	37
The Path to Conscious Change	38

CHAPTER 8: THE 3RD LEVEL OF CHANGE – THE PULL (CALL) 41

Conscious Change and Your Purpose	41
Realizing Your Brilliance, Genius, and Calling	42
Calling You Home	43

CHAPTER 9: SUSTAINING CHANGE 45

Change Who?	46
Change What?	47
The Canvas	49
Imprinting	50
Embedded Beliefs	51
Exercise to Rebelief	51

CHAPTER 10: HOW DO I CHANGE? – DISCIPLINE & CONSISTENCY 53

Discipline & Consistency – No Thank You!	53
The Illusion of Freedom	54
Truly Free to Choose	55

CHAPTER 11: HOW DO I CHANGE? – THE A-WORD 57

You Cannot Do it Alone	58

Ten Questions You Need to Answer Before You Commit to Change … 59

The Extraordinary You … 61

PART II: Being Extraordinary … 63

CHAPTER 12: HOW LONG DOES IT TAKE TO BECOME EXTRAORDINARY? … 67

A Nanosecond … 67

Deciding to be Extraordinary … 68

Staying Extraordinary … 68

Not for the Weak of… … 69

CHAPTER 13: EXTRAORDINARY VISION … 71

Three Things that Can Affect Your Vision and What You Can Do About It … 72

CHAPTER 14: EXTRAORDINARY HUMILITY … 75

Exploring Extraordinary Humility … 75

Extraordinary Humility Is… … 75

Money Can't Buy You Love or Self-Worth … 76

Twelve Signs You Are Moving Toward a Heart-Based Humility … 77

CHAPTER 15: EXTRAORDINARY LOVE … 79

Love is Complex … 80

What's Love Got to Do with It? Is it Love that I'm Feeling? … 81

I Love You and My Car … 82

Extraordinary Definition of Love … 82

Outside of Yourself … 83

CHAPTER 16: EXTRAORDINARY LOVE – SELF … 85

Children and Love … 85

What Others Think … 86

It All Begins With… … 87

What Loving Yourself Looks Like … 88

CHAPTER 17: EXTRAORDINARY LOVE – OTHERS … 91

Your Past Predicts Your Future … 92

Loving Yourself is the Gateway to Loving Others … 92

- Excess Baggage Charges ... 93
- Extraordinary Relationships ... 93
- Same Old Song and Dance ... 94
- Beyond Your Comfort Zones – The Way Out! ... 95
- Being Willing and Able ... 95

CHAPTER 18: EXTRAORDINARY WORK ... 97
- L-O-V-E What You Do ... 97
- Loving Who You Do it With – Inside and Out ... 99
- Loving Where You Do It ... 100

CHAPTER 19: EXTRAORDINARY INSIGHT ... 105
- Go to the Mirror, Boy! ... 105
- Seeing More of You So I Can See More of Me ... 107

CHAPTER 20: EMBRACING EXTRAORDINARY RISK ... 109
- Three Factors That Determine Your Propensity to Risk ... 109
- Obstacles – Your Old Nemesis ... 111

CHAPTER 21: EXTRAORDINARY WISDOM ... 115
- Wisdom and the Human Race ... 116
- Wisdom: Your Fundamental Responsibility ... 117
- The Relationship Between Wisdom, Honesty, and Ego ... 118

CHAPTER 22: EXTRAORDINARY HONESTY ... 121
- Seeking the Whole Truth and Nothing but the Truth ... 121
- The Dualistic Mindset ... 122
- Duality and Complex Issues ... 122
- Three Questions to Ask Yourself About Truth and Honesty: ... 124

CHAPTER 23: EXTRAORDINARY THINKING ... 125
- A Most Extraordinary Thinker ... 125
- Black, White, and Gray ... 127
- The Science Behind Blinding Yourself ... 128
- A Place to Start ... 130

CHAPTER 24: EXTRAORDINARY FORGIVENESS ... 133
- A Culture of Resentment ... 133

- Oh, The Stories We Make Up ... 134
- Killing Me Softly ... 135
- Forgiveness – The Path to Freedom ... 136
- Forgiveness and Living an Extraordinary Life ... 136

CHAPTER 25: EXTRAORDINARY FREEDOM - PART I ... 139
- Cinderella Story ... 140
- America the Free ... 141
- Faux Freedom ... 141
- Addictions We Talk About ... 143
- Addictions We Don't Talk About ... 144

CHAPTER 26: EXTRAORDINARY FREEDOM - PART II ... 147
- Breaking Free – Awareness ... 147
- Breaking Free – Questions ... 148
- Twelve Questions to Determine Your Level of Dependency ... 149
- Deciding on the Next Step ... 150

CHAPTER 27: EXTRAORDINARY SOLITUDE ... 153
- A Little Help? ... 154
- An Epiphany ... 155
- I'm Fine ... 155
- You Complete Me ... 156
- Complete Yourself ... 156

CHAPTER 28: AN EXTRAORDINARY LIFE: IS IT YOURS? ... 159
- A Trip Back in Time ... 160
- D-Day ... 160
- The Story ... 161
- An Extraordinary Burden ... 162
- Am I Enough? ... 163

CHAPTER 29: AN EXTRAORDINARY LIFE - FOR REAL ... 165
- Wait for It? ... 165
- Reflections on a Life ... 166
- An Answered Prayer ... 167

    Rosie the Riveter 168
    A Different Kind of Extraordinary 169
    Never Stop 170
    We All Have Blind Spots 170
    A Story of Extraordinary Love 172
CHAPTER 30: WHAT MAKES UP AN EXTRAORDINARY LIFE 173
    I Want Absolutes 173
    Embracing a Bigger Story 174
    Living in Regret 174
    A Million Decisions, A Million Moments 175
EPILOGUE 177
APPENDIX - Q & A 179
RESOURCES 187
ENDNOTES 190

INTRODUCTION

Change begins at the end of your comfort zone.

Roy T. Bennett

When I began writing this book, I shared some of the concepts and ideas with a number of customers, colleagues, and close friends. I even shared some of the content in my weekly leadership blogs. At the time, quite a few folks asked why I was writing a non-business book—a non-leadership-business book, to be specific—because most had come to expect that genre of book from me based on my leadership development programs and coaching.

When I asked why they classified the material as non-business, they said, "You're writing about ego, humility, the human race, love, self-value, relationships, etc. How can that possibly be considered a business book?"

Here's what I told them:

For more than forty years, I have worked with, worked for, coached, been coached by, led, been led by, mentored, been mentored by, humiliated, been humiliated by, idolized, been idolized by, betrayed, been betrayed by (and every other possible example you can think of) businesspeople and business leaders from every walk of life.

I have come to realize there is an immutable law when it comes to leaders:

You cannot be a rotten person and be a great leader.

I know folks who would adamantly disagree with that statement. That's fine. Everyone has their opinion about what makes a great leader. In my previous book, *Extraordinary Results: Mastering the Art of Leading, Coaching & Influencing Others*, I defined a leader as:

A person who influences others to do or to be their best.

Based on that definition, I find it extremely hard to accept that people can bring out the best in others when they are being the worst versions of themselves. It is an integrity issue, and integrity is a core component of being an extraordinary leader.

On the other hand, I have seen some really good people who were very poor leaders for a number of reasons:

1. They never wanted to be a leader in the first place.
2. They took the position because it was the next logical career step.
3. They never understood that being a leader was more about their people and less about them.
4. They were more enamored with the title and the trappings of being a leader rather than the reality of what it means to actually lead others.
5. Most commonly, more than half took a leadership position for the money.

There is a direct correlation between an individual's appetite for self-reflection and humility and their ability to lead. Unconscious, egocentric, entitled people simply show up in the workplace as unconscious, self-centered, entitled leaders or employees. We have all encountered a few of them along the way. I believe in today's society, these types of people are more the norm than the exception. Sadly, it seems they have become what is ordinary, common, and the standard of what you can expect from others.

It will be the *un*-ordinary who rise above because they are able to see and willing to take advantage of more opportunities in life.

Many of us were taught to respect folks in leadership positions. We are supposed to see them as above us and are expected to follow their lead. This is especially true in the political arena and institutions like universities and churches where hierarchies exist, but we all know leaders who have risen to extremely high levels and act like ignorant, narcissistic buffoons! They disrespect others because they are of the belief that they are the center of the universe.

Whether you are building a career path in leadership or not, whatever your personal and professional goals are, you cannot be a rotten person and be great, much less extraordinary, in achieving those goals.

THE PATH TO AN *UN*-ORDINARY JOURNEY BEGINS...

Self-awareness is the first step in becoming *un*-ordinary. When you can embrace a sense of humility, work to dissolve or minimize your ego, and push yourself outside of your comfort zones, you will then be able to visualize and pursue opportunities to not just be *un*-ordinary, but to live an extraordinary life! Whether you choose to be an extraordinary leader or just want to achieve extraordinary results in life, the pathway is the same—inward!

And that is what this book is all about!

If you choose to live an extraordinary life, you will discover an ever-changing, continual process of striving to step beyond your comfort zone in a multitude of areas as you move through life's various stages.

We live in an instantaneous "can't wait, must have it now" culture that tells you this product, app, relationship, television show, vaccine, or government program is going to cure all of your woes and make you happy. We have been conditioned to search for and expect that a single book, event, guru, person, relationship, or YouTube Video will be the magic potion that will instantaneously transform your average, everyday ordinary life into an extraordinary one.

The idea that external factors are your path to nirvana is being pressed into your neuropaths through the constant bombardment of ads. This is why they speak of ads in the number of impressions. The emergence of clickbait and personalized ads in social media has infiltrated every nook, space, and cranny of your tired, over-stimulated brain. You cannot even put gas in your car without being hounded that all you need to be satisfied is a greasy rotisserie hot-dog that has been rolling around in circles on a grill for twelve hours, a Coke, and a smile.

Add in binge-watching Netflix, Hulu, and Amazon Prime along with the catastrophic reporting of even a half-inch of snow, and you will understand the uphill battle to un-ordinary yourself from a culture that breeds conformity. Your ability to disconnect, unhook, and disengage from being ordinary is a never-ending, ongoing process that begins the second you are conceived and ends the second you take your last breath.

A PROCESS, NOT A DESTINATION

The truth is that leading and living an extraordinary life doesn't happen overnight. Consider, for example, lottery winners who are now poor and unhappy. Or read the memoirs of broken Hollywood actors whose lives behind the facades and the fame were filled with various forms of addiction, escapism, and misery.

Living an extraordinary life doesn't happen instantaneously, and neither is it a place where you arrive.

My life has been a process of constantly unfolding over time. When I was ready, the teacher appeared, the event that transformed me (albeit painful) occurred, and I moved a bit closer to living the life I wanted.

I find, as with most things, that the simpler the idea, the more truth it holds.

If you are an unhappy, dissatisfied person at home and in life, you will be an unhappy, dissatisfied person in the workplace. Unhappy people wreak havoc in the workplace because they are unwilling to accept 100 percent of the responsibility for the results they are creating in their lives.

Why? Because they don't or won't possess the level of self-awareness required to take ownership of their issues. Instead, they deflect and project their problems, inadequacies, and overall unhappiness onto everyone around them. All this happens because deep down within themselves, they are unhappy. They just don't or won't own it.

The fact that most people spend a minimum of 25 percent of their time at work, interacting with more people than they do at home, creates an incredible opportunity to transform the workplace into their very own giant 3D IMAX screen. Here, they can project their garbage on a whole lot more people, issues, and circumstances. In fact, right now, you are probably thinking of the many folks at work who spin endlessly in a circle of toxic gossip, complaining, and misery. Of course, if the work screen isn't big enough to hold their discontentment, they can project their junk onto the government, churches, other countries, races, and religions. One's discontentment and/or fear is at the core of every type of "ism"—racism, sexism, fascism, etc.

We all experience unhappy people every single day. Whether it is at home with our immediate and extended families, our friends, at church, on social media, in the news, and everywhere we go, they are there. In the workplace, this discontentment shows up in poor morale, low engagement, diminished productivity, silos, cliques, social and racial bias, turnover, absenteeism, and favoritism. The cost to the bottom-line is staggering. In life, these unhappy people show up in broken relationships, addictions, crime, the cancel culture, videotaping themselves making a disturbance on an airplane and then posting it on social media, etc.

"So, Joe, what kind of book is this?"

It is a business book, a leadership book, a partial autobiography, a drama, a love story, and a mystery. It is part fiction, part non-fiction, and based on and inspired by real-life events, although names may have been changed to protect the guilty and the innocent.

It was written for you if you are willing to look inward and lean in so far that you can never go back.

Why? Because this is how you gain focus and clarity on what you want, where you want to go, and what is preventing you from getting there.

This book is all about *you* discovering *your* path out of the ordinary and into the extraordinary for the rest of your life! The end goal is to live a life you can say without any doubt is extraordinary, so you can one day leave this world knowing you achieved more than you ever could have imagined possible!

It is an ongoing process that requires a commitment *for life*…your life!

Let's begin...

PART I

CHAPTER 1
THE CHALLENGE TO BE UN-ORDINARY

*Can you remember who you were, before the
world told you who you should be?*

Charles Bukowski

My favorite movie of all time is the 1990 film, *Awakenings*, starring Robin Williams and Robert DeNiro. It is an extraordinary, true story based on the memoirs of Oliver Sacks, a British-born neurologist who discovers a group of post encephalitis patients in a New York hospital. For the most part, they have fallen asleep, transformed from human beings into lifeless statues as an after effect of having the disease. All of them are stone-like, seemingly without thought or emotions. At one point in the movie, Sacks—played by Robin Williams—asks the doctor who found them originally about a particular male patient, "What goes on inside his mind? Is he thinking?"

"Of course not," the neurologist replies.

"Why not?" says Williams.

"Because the implications would be unthinkable!"

The movie takes a turn when Sacks experiments on Leonard Lowe (De Niro) with a drug used to treat Parkinsonian patients called L-DOPA.

The results are nothing short of extraordinary as Leonard awakens and starts to slowly return to a somewhat normal life…for now. Of course, they experiment with other patients, and overnight, the entire group awakens. It is the summer of 1969, which came to be known as "the Awakening."

Eventually, the efficacy of the drug begins to diminish, and Leonard slowly returns to his previous stone-like state. Only now, Sacks knows there is a person, awake, deep down inside of this stone-like figure. The impact of Leonard's awakening on Sacks is an awakening in and of itself.

TIME TO WAKE UP

There are so many different messages and lessons to be learned from this film. For me, one of the greatest takeaways is how each non-afflicted person in the film had been lulled asleep. Life had become ordinary, repetitive, and common. They were sleepwalking through work and through life.

It wasn't until those who had been afflicted with the disease woke up, that those around them were awakened. Sometimes we need those who have the least to remind us of what we need the most.

The unafflicted were awakened to the fact that we take so much for granted, such as our relationships, health, partners, children, and all that we have, such as our ability to walk, think, talk, love, and express ourselves.

Why is it almost always a tragedy in our lives or in the lives of others that must happen for most of us to wake up?

WHAT WE WERE TAUGHT INSTEAD

Most of us were not conditioned to believe that we can live or achieve an extraordinary life. In fact, I think many of us were taught the opposite—to play it safe and seek what was comfortable or ordinary while conforming to the cultural mores.

We were told that pain was bad, and we must avoid it at all costs, even if it meant denying the reality of a situation. We learned to run and hide from pain and suffering, seeking solace or relief in some temporary form of distraction.

We forget or do not accept that our greatest lessons in life would be the remnants left over once we moved through the pain to the other side.

When I was twenty-two years old, my then eighty-four-year-old Sicilian grandmother sat me down to teach me what she believed was an extraordinary life. Not the birds and the bees, mind you, but what steps I needed to take to be extremely happy.

She said, "A-Joey, you go-a to-a da school, get an-a education. Then-a you-a graduate, get-a good-a job, find-a nice-a girl, get-a married, and-a make-a da babies!"

While Grandma's dream might be perfect for somebody, that wasn't me. It wasn't my path nor my dream. We all know folks who followed someone else's path instead of walking their own and are now unfulfilled or miserable.

We all know folks who played it safe and ended up as Thoreau stated, "leading lives of quiet desperation." They get comfortable, settle in, and sleepwalk their way through life.

You can live an extraordinary life. You just have to get perfectly clear on what that looks like for you, not for anyone else. To do that, let's define the word so we can weave it more intricately into our lives.

DEFINING EXTRAORDINARY

To understand the meaning of a word, it is important to first understand the root of its origination. "Extra" literally means "outside." "Ordinary" means "order" and "what is common, comfortable, or known."

CHAPTER 1

When we describe something as "ordinary," we perceive its value to be no longer new or exciting. The newness wears off and it becomes common.

Think of the first time you drove that new car—the smell and the way it handled. You noticed all the little idiosyncrasies, and it was exciting. Then remember what happened when you received the first ding or chip in the windshield. At first, you were angry, and then you cared a little less after each and every ding thereafter. Slowly, it just became another car that you drove for a while. It became ordinary until the next one.

When we label something as extraordinary, it is beyond what we know, believe, do, understand, possess, experience, or feel. Unfortunately, we see the extraordinariness of others more than we see it in ourselves. We idolize folks who are extremely athletic, talented, beautiful, wealthy, handsome, smart, and/or attractive. We label them as being extraordinary or living an extraordinary life.

When we turn the mirror inward and see ourselves, we rarely—if ever—label ourselves as extraordinary. If we do and speak it outwardly, we are seen as arrogant or delusional. We have learned that others can deem us worthy of being extraordinary, but we cannot deem ourselves worthy of this label.

The truth is, when it comes to ourselves, we all have an opportunity to live an extraordinary life if we are willing to go outside of what is comfortable, common, and known to us. This means living an extraordinary life is extremely personal.

IT'S YOUR BUSINESS AND IT'S PERSONAL

Your thoughts and beliefs are very personal to you. Even though you may share your beliefs with others, no one can experience it exactly the way you do. No one can be inside your head, which means that no one will ever fully experience, understand, or comprehend your world. No one gets you better than you.

Sure, you can compare yourself to others, but that takes away the mystery and uniqueness that makes each and every one of us *extraordinary*!

You make "extraordinary" your own by being self-aware enough to know when you are moving outside of *your* common, *your* ordinary, *your* comfortable. This mindset requires that you constantly change.

Ironically, most people fear change, so they do the exact opposite. They seek out what gives them a sense of safety, albeit a false sense. They seek a sense of belonging instead of standing alone. We refer to this as *herd mentality*.

When your need to belong supersedes your need to be extraordinary, you limit your ability to lead an extraordinary life. You stall, stop, coast, and blend in. You lose your individuality, and worse, you lose what is so unique about you. You lose your brilliance, your genius, and your extraordinary.

No one I know was ever praised or recognized for being extraordinarily common. The history books are not filled with common people. It is the extraordinary people whom we want to write about and remember.

These are the folks who risked, going outside what they knew or what others believed to be true and known. They pushed their envelope and embraced their need to go beyond, coupling it with their willingness to embrace change to move forward toward their purpose—their calling in life.

It is, was, and continues to be the road not taken:

> *Two roads diverged in a wood, and I—*
> *I took the one less traveled by,*
> *And that has made all the difference.*
>
> **Robert Frost**

CHAPTER 1

STILL WANT TO BE EXTRAORDINARY?

At this point, you have three possible options. You might think about committing to one of these pathways:

Path A: Stay put and do nothing, even though it might be unfulfilling or somewhat uncomfortable. It's not *so* uncomfortable that you want to change, but just uncomfortable enough to keep you there (wherever it is that you've stalled). It sometimes feels like a constant dull ache that is telling you that something isn't quite right, something is missing, or you're missing the mark. You have a solid justification (rational or not) as to why you need to stay where you are. You're fine!

This isn't why you picked up this book, is it? You definitely have a choice to put down the book and go back to normal, or you can keep reading.

Path B: You take a baby step forward and put your toe in the water. Not even the big toe, just the little pinky toe. You're not sure where this is going to take you, but you're willing to look. You've mapped out your emergency exits just in case you want to bail or it begins to get a little too uncomfortable. Yes, they are probably similar to the other exits you've had in place in other similar situations, but you tell yourself, "Well, at least I'm willing to try!"

I don't think this is why you picked up this book either. You're not all the way in, but you're kind of, mostly, sort of in. Better than Path A, so keep reading!

Path C: You throw caution to the wind. You jump in headfirst. You lean in so far that you can't go back! You embrace the idea that you are destined for this path. You realize you will bump into some obstacles—your beliefs, what you know, what you do, what you have been taught, and what you have learned through life's lessons—but you commit to being open to altering all of those things. You are all in! By simply choosing this path, the path less taken, you have taken your first step toward achieving your unique and very personal extraordinary life!

It is time to...

DECIDE!

CHAPTER 2
THE WAKE-UP CALL

Without change, something sleeps inside us, and seldom awakens. The sleeper must awaken.

Frank Herbert, *Dune*

I remember my first real wake-up call. I was eighteen years old and sitting in my Sicilian mother's kitchen. On the harvest gold stove is a giant 350-gallon vat of spaghetti sauce simmering, bubbling, and wafting an incredible aroma throughout the house and into the neighbor's yard. One of my five Uncle Tonys was coming over for dinner and my mother wanted to make sure we didn't run out.

She was in the galley rolling out a pizza crust with her head down, having all the intensity of a bull running through the streets of Pamplona. She didn't utter a word, only an occasional grunt as she rolled the dough into a flattened state. I was certain she wished and even pictured my head under the rolling pin instead of the dough!

I was seated at the kitchen table, stoned out-of-my-mind. I had just completed my freshman year at *Thee* Ohio State University, and on the table in front of me is my report card. In very small, black type under GPA, which in my state of mind looked more like eight feet tall numbers blinking in green neon, were the results of my less-than-stellar performance for my first year away from home.

G-P-A: 1.35

The reason my mom was so upset was that she knew I was a mess. I skipped class, screwed around, and partied like Keith Richards after a transfusion. I spent the majority of my time drinking, getting high, and exploring my co-ed floor in my co-ed dorm. I was your basic burned-out pot head on a collision course toward being kicked out of school. I was so very lost!

THE ALARM GOES OFF – TIME TO WAKE UP

My mom put down her rolling pin, turned to me, took a step forward and said, "You know something Joey?"

I'm quite stoned, so I answered, "Ummm, like… Uhhh, what?"

She said, "I am angry, and I am sad! I am angry because you have a brother who is developmentally challenged and wishes he could do half the things that you can, but he can't! And I am sad, because you have all the God-given talent in the world and you are wasting your life!"

She then leans in real close, so close I can feel her anger masking the tears forming in the corners of her eyes. She is in my face when she screams, "When are you going to *wake up*?!"

Now when your mother is Sicilian, five-foot-ten, and has a rolling pin and a sharp knife within her reach, oh, believe me, you wake up!

WHO'S DEVELOPMENTALLY CHALLENGED?

Now, here was my brother Billy struggling through life, being ridiculed and taunted daily, and yet he was still doing the best he could. As you know, people can be cruel, and back then, the way we treated people with disabilities was an abomination. In some ways, even today we still do not treat them well.

And there I was, a burned-out pothead on a path to throwing my life away. Again, sometimes we need those with less to show us what it is we need most.

So based on what I've told you up to this point, you tell me who was the developmentally- challenged one?

But you see, my mom was right. I needed to wake up! I had fallen into a deep sleep, and I desperately needed to be woken up. If I am being honest, I must admit that I don't know if I had ever been awake up to that point in my life. I think like most kids, I was trying to just fit in and be cool.

For some reason, I must have been ready to wake up because her words stuck. They impacted me at a soul-level, and they started me down a path of discovery filled with a whole lot of questions!

QUESTIONS, QUESTIONS, AND MORE QUESTIONS!

Who was I? Why was I here? What was I supposed to be doing with my life? What was my purpose?

That wake-up call didn't answer any of these questions, but it sent me down a path to start asking those questions and searching for answers. I decided to take a step down a much different path from the one I had been walking.

My life has never been the same.

As I have journeyed through life, I have found myself at various times moving through an up-and-down roller-coaster journey, falling asleep in one area and waking up in another. This is a critical point to remember for much later in the book.

When I am asleep, I am typically avoiding some-*thing*, some-*one*, some-

situation, or some-*issue* in my life. Sometimes it is an unconscious choice, and at other times it is not. It is a clear choice to avoid or suppress.

Once you wake up regarding an issue in your life, it can be hard to stay asleep for long because you now know you're choosing to avoid it. It is like being an alcoholic and going to AA meetings for a while. It ruins your ability to drink freely ever again because of the pang of guilt, knowing you are choosing to do something you shouldn't. It simply eats at you—either that, or the pain of your actions (inactions) comes roaring back and knocks you on your ass.

Pain is the world's greatest alarm clock because it provides you with one of two options.

- **Option 1:** Hit the snooze button, roll over, and fall back asleep, pretending you don't have to get up because there really isn't anything wrong.
- **Option 2:** Wake up, plant your feet on the floor, and stand up and face the day, the issue, the person, the discomfort, etc.

When I am awake, I am conscious, intentional, and aligned with my purpose and who I know I am. It has been and continues to be some of the most productive times in my life, but not because there is incredible movement forward or a massive amount of activity. It is because I am choosing to move beyond what is outside of what is or was comfortable, known, or safe.

Sometimes that means sitting in the discomfort for a while. It could be a day, a week, a month, or even a year. Other times, it means persistent and consistent activity. Mostly, it is a combination of both, knowing when and how long to sit, and knowing when to get up and move.

It is time to…

WAKE UP!

CHAPTER 3
ARE YOU SURE YOU WANT TO WAKE UP?

> *This is your last chance. After this there is no turning back. You take the blue pill, the story ends; you wake up in your bed and believe whatever you want to believe.*
>
> **From the Movie *The Matrix***

In the popular 1999 science fiction movie, *The Matrix*, Neo (Keanu Reeves), a highly-skilled computer hacker by night who hides behind his day job as a mild-mannered software programmer, meets Morpheus. Pay attention to the names here—Neo, which means "new," and Morpheus, meaning "to change form."

Morpheus (Laurence Fishburne), the head of a cyber-rebellion, is explaining to Neo what he already knows deep inside of him but has failed to identify. The world is false, and it doesn't exist. It is an actual matrix where everyone is asleep.

Morpheus believes that Neo is the one to lead the charge and defeat the enemy who is hell-bent on keeping the world asleep and unconscious.

Early on in the movie, during their first meeting, a conversation ensues between Neo and Morpheus where Morpheus gives Neo a big old fat reality check, along with a life-changing decision he must make. He must choose the blue pill or the red pill.

Take the blue pill and the story ends, and he can go back to sleep in his own bed back home, where it is safe, known, and comfortably uncomfortable!

Take the red pill and he stays awake in this new, unknown, seemingly unsafe world. Just like Alice, this is Wonderland and Morpheus wants to show him just how deep the rabbit hole goes.

"Rabbit hole" refers to a bizarre, confusing, unknown, uncertain world where when one chooses that path, it is difficult, if not impossible to remove oneself. It is in reference to Lewis Carroll's book, *Alice in Wonderland*, published in 1865 and later made famous by Disney's 1951 movie adaptation.

Should you decide to go down the rabbit hole, you enter a freefall, alternate space where you are outside of reality that you have known and clung to all your life. It is the point of no return.

It is a decision to stay asleep or to wake up—wake up to a new (neo) reality and transform (morph) into something new, different, or better, as in the best version of yourself.

THE COST OF LIVING YOUR LIFE ASLEEP

Emerson's Law of Compensation basically states that there is a universal law of adjustment and compensation, otherwise known as a universal balancing system. It implies that adding effort into one area of your life will deduct it from another area of your life.

For example, if you stay at work longer to finish a presentation, it will cost you time with your family, which seems straight forward and simple. Where this trips people up is when they fail to see that, because they are blind, unaware, or unconscious of an area that is being negatively impacted in their life.

A married client of mine and his wife have a twenty-six-year-old daughter. Their daughter's best friend, who spends a good deal of time at their house, drives my client absolutely nuts.

He is a thirty-year-old unmotivated, unemployed young man who doesn't want to work. He says that he does, but instead, he lives at home with his mother, plays video games, and collects unemployment.

If you ask him what his plans are, he will tell you that he is preparing to go to Community College sometime in the near future—approximately 8 months in the future. He is lost, and more importantly, he is asleep. He is unaware that his inactions and reliance on the government are basically robbing him of his potential, his future, and his opportunity to live an extraordinary life.

Author Joan Welsh said it best: "If you're coasting, you're either losing momentum or else you're headed downhill." Coasting is easy, does not require effort, hard work, or uncomfortableness, initially. It does, however, cost you eventually.

Every check he collects unconsciously strips another day, month, or year from his dignity, self-respect, and more importantly, his ability to live a meaningful life. This is not about blaming or condemning. A lot of folks are in the same place. It is not out of stupidity; it is out of *ignorance*. He is ignoring the long-term, inevitable damage to his sense of self. It is a different rabbit hole of sorts, only instead of finding his new (neo) self, he is losing his entire sense of self. The problem is that the longer you sleep, the more painful it becomes to wake up. It is just easier to go back to sleep.

IS IGNORANCE REALLY BLISS?

We have all the heard the phrase, "Ignorance is bliss." We may experience people who are totally oblivious to the world around them, and we think to ourselves, "Wow! Wouldn't it be nice to not have a care in the world? To go through life seemingly happy and unaware?"

There are three problems with this mindset:

1. You never wake up and never fully live life the way it was intended because you are living in only one-half of reality.
2. You eventually wake up, but it is too late and you are overwhelmed by an immense feeling of regret. Most deathbed confessions or regrets can attest to this.
3. You and the world miss out on your genius and your brilliance. You never experience the sheer joy of leveraging your unique gifts in a way that serves a purpose greater than yourself. The world misses out because they never experience your brilliance, your genius, and your giftedness.

If you want to live an extraordinary life, you must accept the innumerable truth that life, at times, will be difficult.

HELICOPTERS AND LAWN MOWERS

Unfortunately, we have been teaching the last few generations of children that life should be easy. I'm not saying we should intentionally make it hard or cause them to suffer. Life will deal them enough challenges and pains. I am saying we should not protect them from the reality of life, but we do!

We are all familiar with the term Helicopter Parent. These are parents who hover over their children and swoop in to save them at the first sign of trouble.

We now have a new breed of parent, referred to as "Lawnmower Parents."[1] These are parents who, like lawnmowers, attempt to cut down any obstacles that could potentially stand in their child's way. They will do whatever they must do to remove adversity, struggle or failure that is in their child's path, real or perceived. In doing so, they create a false comfort zone for their children the size of the state of Texas. It is so big and so comfortable, why would anyone ever want to leave?

Children choose a sport or hobby and quit at the first sign of difficulty. They would rather master the art of sitting in front of a large screen with a controller in their hands, playing games in a virtual world, instead of living and experiencing the real one.

To believe that you or your children can escape all the difficulties, uncomfortableness, or pain in life is simply not realistic. Protecting them from the realities of life actually does more damage than good. When you do that, you send them into the world unprepared and unable to navigate it, teaching them to be dependent on others for their well-being, which includes where they get their sense of self-worth and value.

The truth is that every second of every day, life is unfolding in a natural ebb and flow of opposites. The transition between day and night, the contrast of black and white, and the movement between periods of happiness and sadness are just a few examples of the ongoing, ever-changing cycle of life. This is life. This is reality.

If you want to live an extraordinary life, you must wake up to the reality that life includes embracing both the comfortable and the uncomfortable. Ignoring the existence of either side of the equation will cause you to be lulled asleep.

Waking up requires that you change.

EMBRACING CHANGE

Living life fully awake and conscious means you will be required to change. It has been said over and over that people do not like change. While this isn't true for everyone, I believe that the more conscious and awake you are, the more willing you are to embrace change.

However, a lot of folks choose to stay asleep. They despise change because it disrupts their sleeping patterns. Change means that things are going to get uncomfortable at times. It means they will have to step outside of their comfort zones and go beyond what is known, safe, and secure. This can be difficult, especially if they have worked hard to tuck themselves into a nice, cozy, warm, comfortable bed that they created.

Unfortunately, the world prefers that you stay asleep. Companies like Google, Amazon, and Facebook would prefer that you never leave your home. They would prefer that you sit at home, click on ads, buy services and products online, and keep searching so they can continue to profit.

The government, religious institutions, and the media would prefer that you trust them and follow blindly. To do that, you must be asleep and dependent on them. That is how they continue to exist without providing any real value.

If you were to take one thing from this entire book, this is it:

YOU, and only you, are 100 percent responsible for the results you are getting in your life.

This includes the life-defining decision to coast through life asleep or walk through life awake.

If you are willing to embrace this belief and accept 100 percent responsibility for your life, then you are ready for the next step. You must choose the red pill and go down the rabbit hole. You must willingly embrace the uncertainty and allow yourself to morph into the best version of yourself. The extraordinary you. The *neo* you!

It is time to…

CHANGE!

CHAPTER 4
THE THEORY OF NON-CHANGEABILITY (INFLEXIBILITY)

Everyone thinks of changing the world, but no one thinks of changing himself.

Leo Tolstoy

Practically everyone has heard of Einstein's Theory of Relativity and the infamous equation, $E=mc^2$. It translates into energy equals mass times the speed of light squared. This might be somewhat hard to comprehend, especially if you are not scientifically inclined. The point to remember is that it is about forces of nature at work.

When it comes to change there are also forces of nature at work—human nature.

While it is next to impossible to change mother nature, it is almost equally as hard to shift human nature—not because we can't, but because we won't. In my coaching work with leaders, one of the most powerful questions to ask people when they say they can't do something is, "Is it because you can't or because you won't?" Big difference, and it totally shifts the conversation!

Over the course of many years working with people, I have realized that the biggest obstacle blocking most people's inability to change is their ego.

THE EGO

The ego has been described in many ways: the small self, the false self, self-image, psyche, pride, vanity, subconscious, selfishness, self-importance, pride, false pride, arrogance, personality, narcissism, vainness, the big I, the little i, vainglory, individuality, self-worth, conceit, anima, and inner self.

Ego has caused the demise of more leaders, countries, dictators, personal relationships, marriages, businesses, business relationships, careers, and families than any other factor known to mankind. In most situations if you were to peel back the onion, you will find an overinflated ego. Just like an onion, it usually stinks and/or will bring you to tears.

Though we are aware of this phenomenon, it continues to be a dis-*ease*[2] that infects the world on an individual and global level. If you don't believe me, simply spend a few hours on Facebook or any other social media outlet.

In contrast, all the great teachers taught about this issue. Buddha, Jesus, St Francis of Assisi, Martin Luther, Confucius, Krishna, Gandhi, the Dalai Lama, Mandela, and Martin Luther King speak to and demonstrate how they lived their lives, dissolving their ego.

YOUR EGO

Your ego attempts to stay hidden in your subconscious. It hides there in the background so you can believe it is your true self. The problem is that the ego believes it is you and you believe you are your ego.

It is my belief that the ego was formed to protect your sense of self. Most of us did not grow up in extraordinarily healthy environments or with the healthiest self-images. We were taught that our sense of self-worth and value comes from external factors, those being outside of our selves.

These factors include our parents, peers, teachers, pastors, rabbi, nuns, the media, the government, the church, and companies who advertise their products as solutions designed to make us feel good about ourselves and to foster some sense of worth and value.

There is an inverse relationship between self-worth and ego. The lower your internal sense of self-worth, the larger your ego. The higher your inner sense of self-worth and value, the less of an ego you will have.

It is important to note the difference between confidence and arrogance, between pride and false pride, and between ego and healthy self-esteem. It is also important to clarify that ego in and of itself is not a bad thing. It is there to protect our sense of self-worth and value. It is a defense mechanism to fend off perceived assaults on the self. The more fragile the inner sense of self, the bigger the ego needs to be, and so too the level of self-inflation.

Think of your self-worth as an inner tube. If it is flat or leaking, it requires a constant influx of air to keep it inflated. The problem is that while you are inflating your ego to be seen as good enough, smart enough, right enough, successful enough, or likable enough, it is having the direct opposite results on how others see and experience you.

Healthy people don't see you as smart, wonderful, successful, or want to be around you more if you don't have a good sense of self-worth. They will see you as small, ignorant, and a loser. They won't like you, nor will they want to be around you, which is the exact opposite result that you think you are achieving from inflating yourself.

There is a saying about egocentric people. "They are so full of themselves!" This actually makes sense because you are attempting to inflate yourself to appear bigger or larger than life while you hold your own air hose.

MY SUPREME COURT

I think the best description for one's ego is an internal judicial system or a courtroom of sorts. In your courtroom, you get to play the judge, jury, prosecutor, defense attorney, bailiff, and even the court stenographer. While the stenographer doesn't seem to be an important position, it allows you to transcribe the proceeding in a way that you want to remember it, the way you need to make the story fit your internal dialogue, again and again.

I am quite confident I am not the only person who can relate to this. As I replay an incident over in my mind where I felt disrespected, scorned, belittled, or less than, I slam down the gavel each and every time, shouting, "Guilty! Guilty as charged!" I then hand out the sentence or punishment in some form of dismissal, banishment, belittlement, condemnation, or gossip. At the heart of this matter is my inherent need to prove two egocentric beliefs.

In borrowing from Einstein, I have come up with an equation for the ego:

$$E = rc^2$$

Where:

- E = ego
- r = my need to be right, and
- c^2 = my need to be in control.

EGOIC THEORY AND THE NEED TO BE RIGHT

There is a huge buzz of electricity when I slam down the gavel and prove myself right and the other party wrong. I get a sense of power from controlling everyone in the courtroom, albeit a false sense of power. Because I am also in control of the facts, that allows me to justify my beliefs as well as my actions.

THE THEORY OF NON-CHANGEABILITY (INFLEXIBILITY)

The need to be right and the need to be in control serve two purposes. As humans, the need to be right is driven by our desire to see everything in an either/or way. We will talk more about this in much more detail in the later chapters. For now, let's just call it black-and-white thinking.

If I am right, you must be wrong. If I win, you must lose. If I am smart, you must be dumb, or at least I must be smarter than you. Our ego thrives on this either-or thinking because it puts me in the good pile and you in the bad pile. It is a way of inflating my sense of self. Again, the lower the inner sense of self-worth, the more right I need to be, the more I must win, the more I must control, the more…, etc. You get the picture.

EGOIC THEORY AND THE NEED TO BE IN CONTROL

Working in partnership with my need to be right is my need to be in control. I believe this plays into part of my need to feel safe and secure. This is why so many people feel afraid when they are face-to-face with forces beyond their control. Think of being in an earthquake. The ground is shaking violently, things are crashing to the ground, and you have absolutely no control over mother nature.

Control is not a bad thing. Where it becomes a problem is when and where we attempt to control things we have absolutely no control over. The truth is we really don't have control over most things. In fact, the only thing we have control over is what we think. Carl Jung, the great psychoanalyst, would add: "It is not what it is, it is what we make things mean."

If I am not in control, I am vulnerable, I could lose, I could be publicly embarrassed, and I could be seen as small, inadequate, stupid, ignorant, petty, or fake. If I cannot control others or the situation, I might be hurt physically, emotionally, or mentally.

This is where human nature steps in to protect us. This is where the ego comes in to protect our sense of self and bring about a feeling of safety and security.

If we were to unravel this illusion of control, we would see that we are holding on tightly to a false sense of safety and security. It is not real. Remember the scene from *The Matrix* between Morpheus and Neo? If you choose the red pill, you go down the rabbit hole. If you choose the blue pill, you go back to sleep.

Moving beyond this false state to a more accurate picture of reality requires letting go of what you don't control and realizing what you do. This may sound simple, but it is not easy, and it requires an immense amount of mature wisdom.

Maybe Alcoholics Anonymous has it right when they recite the Serenity Prayer:

Grant me the serenity (security & peace),

to accept the things I cannot change,

the courage to change the things I can (myself & my thoughts),

and the wisdom to know the difference.

CHAPTER 5
DIS-SOLVING THE EGO

You must choose not to judge the object in any way, attach to it, reject it as meaningless, like it or dislike it. This is merely the need of the ego to categorize and control and define itself by preferences.

Richard Rohr, *The Naked Now*

YOUR EGO DOES NOT WANT TO BE DIS-SOLVED

Imagine you are standing on top of a very tall building in downtown Chicago. Standing to the left of you is a person you do not know very well—you only know them based on what you have heard or read about them. You have sought them out because you have a need—a desire to live a more fulfilled and free life. You want to trust them, but there is a certain amount of doubt and uncertainty.

They lean over and whisper in your ear that if you want to be free, if you want to really live, if you want to experience an extraordinary life, you must jump off the building. There is no net, no bungee cord, and no strings or ropes attached. You cannot quite comprehend how you could survive the jump, but a part of you knows you need to jump and trust the process.

On the other side of you is someone else who has been with you as far back as you can remember. Never once have they left your side or abandoned you, even though at times you felt lost or abandoned. You know and trust them, though they have created some very painful experiences in your life. They have damaged more than a few relationships with both family and friends, they've cost you a marriage, they were at the core of a few bad financial decisions, and they were the source of a few missed career opportunities.

You keep them around because they serve a purpose in your life, to protect you and your sense of self-worth at all costs, even though it is not the real you but a false you. They are screaming in your other ear, telling you that if you jump, you are dead and will cease to exist. You will be a big nothing, a nada, a zero, a zed, a splat, a squish and then gone!

So to whom do you listen? Which advice do you take? Do you jump or stay put? Do you fly or stay grounded? Do you take the red pill or the blue pill?

LIFE IS FILLED WITH PARADOX

That is what it feels like to be faced with the decision to dissolve the ego. What makes this so challenging is that your ego believes it is you, and you believe you are your ego. Letting go, or jumping, most certainly feel like death. Like so many of life's paradoxes, we must die to live (figuratively speaking), we must lose our lives to find our lives, in the same way we must let go to hold onto, give to receive, fail to succeed. The more you resist, the more it (whatever it is) persists, etc.

The truth is that most of us have no idea who we are separate from the image our mind creates for us, the image that has been forming within us in our subconscious for our entire lives. Without our ego, we are nothing, and our biggest fear is being a nothing. We have probably felt this way about ourselves more times than we care to admit, which is why we have to inflate ourselves and prop up our self-image. It is the proverbial Catch-22.

The truth about you, is that even though you realize you are not your ego, your ego will flat out reject that idea. Your ego is going to fight like hell to not die. It may appear to give in and then attack you when your defenses are down.

Dissolving the ego means you must know when your ego is taking the wheel and driving the bus. That requires you to be totally vigilant, conscious, awake and alert!

REDUCING THE EGO – PART I

In mathematics, to reduce a number, we must divide it by another number or another factor. (Ex: 16 ÷ 4 = 4, 4 ÷ 4 = 1, and so on.) The same theory applies to the ego. To reduce the ego, we must divide it by another factor.

The following equation illustrates how this might happen:

$$e = E/Ah^2$$

Where:

- e = the reduced ego
- E = the inflated ego or false self
- A = acceptance of what is
- h^2 = humility

It is in the acceptance—not needing to always be right and not having to prove you are smart or worthy—that reduces the big E. It is in the acceptance of what is, of knowing that you can only ever control yourself, your thoughts, and your actions. Thinking you can control others is an illusion and is probably adding to your problems, your dis-ease, and the size of your ego.

We must be wise enough to accept what is, not what we want, wish, or hoped it would be. Some folks will see this as giving up, quitting, surrendering, or throwing in the towel. They didn't achieve the level of success they have by sitting on their ass and letting life and opportunity pass them by. They will tell you they didn't succeed because they accepted the status quo.

Let me clarify. I am not saying to give up exerting effort or trying to change. I am also not saying don't strive to have nice things if that is what you want. What I am saying is two-fold:

- Stop trying to change or control what you can't. This includes other people, the past, factors outside of your influence, or the future.
- Cut the umbilical cord between your value and self-worth from the level of effort. Detach your sense of self-worth and value from the price tag you pay, the toys you have, the amount of money in the bank, the number of initials after your name, who you know, and the label you wear on the outside of your clothes. The labels on the outside do not indicate the value of what is on the inside.

Acceptance is the key to learning to lead an extraordinary life regardless of what life sends your way with all its twists and turns, and acceptance is only the first half of the equation.

REDUCING THE EGO – PART II

The other factor in the equation is the ever-evasive, hard-to-swallow factor in the equation known as humility. We talk about humility a great deal. Many of the great teachers were oozing humility, and I think a lot of people often confuse humility with humiliation. It is important to understand the difference.

Humility is derived from the Latin word, *humilis*, which means "low."

Years ago, in an act of humility, a person, or subject (as in the king's subject) would lie face down on the ground, arms stretched out and legs together simulating a cross at the feet of a nobility or clergy. This act of prostration was the ultimate form of humility and respect.

The king was elevated a few feet above the ground on a throne while you lowered yourself as low as you could go, to the earth. The Latin noun *humus* means "earth" and is the very word from which the Latin adjective *humilis* derives.

Nowadays, it rarely happens where we literally humble ourselves on the ground. Today, it is very much a figurative interpretation of the word.

HUMILITY

When I choose to lower myself instead of raising myself above others, I am choosing humility. I do this by trying to understand their needs before my own and seeking to understand before trying to be understood.

Taking the focus from myself and my needs is so much more difficult to do than to simply lie on the ground and fake humility for a few minutes. The former requires a continuous monitoring of my ego, knowing that I have nothing to prove to the other party. I have no need to inflate my sense of self, to be right, or in control, so I am perfectly willing to lower myself. My sense of self is not based on external factors because I am secure in knowing who I am. I know I have value and worth.

HUMILIATION

When I intentionally attempt to ridicule others, prove they are wrong, insult them, retaliate, or make them feel lesser than me, I am choosing to humiliate them. It is my attempt to inflate and raise myself while attempting to lower the other person. Of course, this is all in my mind and isn't real. It is the ego's way of making me feel important, better than, or at least not less than.

We can choose to be humble (lower ourselves) or we can choose to humiliate (lower others). It is an internal versus external locus of control.

At some point in our lives, we have all experienced some form of humili ation, whether it was as a child, an awkward adolescent as we were trying to find where we belonged, a love relationship gone bad, or at work.

Realizing the difference between doing something wrong and being something wrong has been described as the difference between guilt and shame. Guilt says *we did* something bad; shame says *we are* bad. Big difference.

If we believe we are bad, wrong, defective, stupid, unworthy, of little value, etc., we will have to inflate our ego in some way, shape, or form to compensate for the feelings of inadequacy. If we accept that we are not perfect, that we are human, and that we will make bad decisions at times, we may be more apt to be humble than if we are not.

We have introduced the concept of embracing humility and will revisit what living with extraordinary humility might look like a bit later in the book.

The ego is the biggest factor getting in the way of your ability to embrace change. Once we become aware of just how dominant our ego is in our quest to feel some sense of worth, we can go to work on dissolving or reducing its impact on our lives and those around us.

Once we diminish the obstacle of our ego, we are ready to begin embracing change. Understanding the different types of change and the impact they have on our lives is the next step in this transformational process as we move toward living a life that is extraordinary!

CHAPTER 6
THE 1ST LEVEL OF CHANGE – THE PUSH

IN THE BEGINNING

When you were approximately twenty-two days old, inside your mother's womb, your heart began to beat. For the previous twenty-one days, a vein that was forming in you began folding over, creating chambers that eventually became your heart.

As a fetus you had to do nothing to make this transformational process unfold. The life force, energy, and source that was pushing your development happened without any effort from you.

The same life force continuing in this exact moment in time is pushing you forward. It is unconscious, involuntary, and happens regardless of whether you believe it or not. It constantly pushes life forward until it doesn't, which means change is taking place and driving us forward whether we want it, fear it, fight it, accept it, embrace it, or do nothing!

SEASONS OF CHANGE

The point to remember is that this type of change—the push, as I have labeled it—does not stop. While the speed or direction may shift, from slow to fast or from expansion to contraction at different times and phases of our life, it doesn't stop until we stop. Some would say it continues long after our physical bodies have life in them. It stops when our life, as we currently know it, comes to an end.

People have attempted to slow this process we label as *aging*. I see it differently because I believe it is much bigger than that. It is a transformation of life.

Many have searched for ways to extend this process with things like the fountain of youth, the Holy Grail, plastic surgery, and Botox. You simply cannot stop this change from moving us forward. You may slow it down, but you cannot stop the natural flow of life. Nothing in life is static. You're either moving forward or you are moving backward.

Some folks believe that there is such a thing as coasting. While it may be true, remember that it probably means you're either losing momentum or headed downhill. You can't coast through life and be more than ordinary.

This is not new thinking. The Greek Philosopher Heraclitus said basically the same thing approximately 2500 years ago, "Everything changes, and nothing stands still." Life doesn't stand still and wait for us! This hard cold fact of life should be cause enough for us to embrace change. Sadly, most of us do not. In fact, in most cases, people resist change, thinking they can prevent it from happening.

I believe this represents one of life's great paradoxes, namely that what we resist persists, and that in certain areas of our life we are driven to change or be changed.

LOOKING OUT THE PICTURE WINDOW OF LIFE

When I reflect on the path of my life, an image comes to mind. I always imagined life beginning for all of us in a tiny, somewhat cramped one-bedroom apartment, where all our needs are met. As tenants, we are housed in this small apartment for nine-months as we grow and develop without much effort of our own.

We are birthed, and this transformational process continues as we develop. We learn to walk, talk, learn, and interact with others. A part of our life changes without much, if any, major effort from us. There are phases of expansion until we reach a tipping point when a period or phase of contractions begins.

At some point, hopefully after many years on this earth, as we near the end of our lives, many of us end up back in a small, compact one-bedroom apartment. Depending on our choices and circumstances, we may have people there to help us and tend to our needs because we may not be able to meet those needs ourselves.

Throughout our entire life, this energy, this life force—or whatever it is you want to label it—is pushing us to the next phase, the next stage, and the next level of life. The question is how to navigate these shifts, because we do have choices. We can fear it, acknowledge but ignore it, fight it, or embrace it.

If we can step back to examine our lives, we will see that this energy is a thread that weaves itself through the all the other levels of change we experience in life.

We need to be conscious and aware that this Level I change plays an important role in the unfolding. In conjunction with Level II and Level III change, it forms the basis for the transformation of life so we can move closer to living a life that we can claim is extraordinary.

EXERCISE: REFLECTION

- Are you awake and aware of this energy or life force that is pushing through change?
- Are you fighting it, fearing it, acknowledging but ignoring it, or are you fully embracing it?
- Are you leveraging this type of change to help you move closer to living your extraordinary life?

CHAPTER 6

Knowing that we are in a constant state of change allows us to leverage this knowledge, using it to help navigate the other levels.

While we can influence this first level of change, we cannot control it. So many things come into play, such as genetics, acts of God, fate, or chance, etc. However, it does play an integral part in the other levels of change we will discuss in the next two chapters.

Level II change is where we can find a tipping point, that can help you discover the critical path toward living an extraordinary life.

CHAPTER 7
THE 2ND LEVEL OF CHANGE – THE PAIN

And the day came when the risk to remain tight in a bud was more painful than the risk it took to blossom.

Anais Nin

CHANGE OR DIE AND LET'S MAKE A DEAL

There are times in life when we feel stuck. For whatever reason, we are paralyzed or immobilized in a situation or circumstance we wish could be different. As a result, we experience varying levels of stress, frustration, discomfort, or pain.

It might be a small speed bump on our path, or it could be a life-defining event that kicks our ass and sets us back on our heels, such as a divorce, or the loss of a parent, spouse, child, or someone dear to us. It could be a career path derailment that blindsides us or a financial crisis that wipes out our sense of security and turns our world upside down.

Any event that causes upheaval for us and makes us question ourselves, our decisions, or what we value most in life can be a guiding light telling us that we are not living the life we want or hope for.

Whatever it is, the pain we feel can drive us to change. The decision to change usually happens when the perceived pain of changing becomes less than the pain we are experiencing in our given situation or predicament.

Sometimes our pain is connected to fear. We may fear not having or at least not seeing a way out of a situation, relationship, or career that seems hopeless. We may feel trapped or at the mercy of something or someone else's influence or decision. Hopeless is the word that comes to mind.

There seems to be a symbiotic relationship between fear, change, and pain. The greater the fear, the greater the pain, and the greater the pain, the greater the change needed to move beyond the current challenge we face.

TEMPORARY QUICKSAND

Unfortunately, the change is often temporary. We change just long enough to quell the pain or feel some bit of relief. We change just enough or just long enough to distance ourselves from the pain, whether it is to prevent our spouse from leaving, quell the urgency of the medical issue, or bury the grief of losing a loved one. Sometimes it is just a matter of allowing enough time to reduce the intensity of the pain without ever really making any serious changes in our lives.

I call this the Quicksand Phase, which is described eloquently in Alan Deutschman's book entitled *Change or Die*.[3] *He shared how patients who received angioplasty (stints in the arteries of the heart to prevent blockage) generally go right back to their old destructive behaviors once the danger of dying has subsided. The idea is that even when faced with death, the change is only temporary.*

What is it about us humans, that once the threat of death passes or we experience a reduction in pain, we simply slide right back into our old pattern, which is usually the same pattern that created the pain in the first place?

It is as if we are awakened and then slowly fall back asleep until the same problem rears its ugly head again, or a seemingly different problem (a deriva-

tive of the original) shows up on our radar screen, and we once again must be jarred awake.

It is analogous to the beginning of a bad relationship. All the red flags are there, you see them, you ignore them, and you push them down and pretend they are not there. Think about downhill skiers in the Olympics. They are going so fast and coming so close to the flags that they actually knock them over on their way down as if they are not there!

We do the same thing; we ignore all the warning signs as we walk through life unconscious and asleep. We intentionally ignore, run over, and blow past the signs that tell us we must change. Of course, by ignoring them, we end up wiping out, hitting a wall, or are so backed into a corner there is only one way out—change!

The shift that happens once we decide to change can be transformational. We become laser-like in our focus and attention to face the issue and resolve it. Again, just like in Deutschman's description of how angioplasty patients become diligent in changing behavior right up to the point of surgery when the angel of death is knocking on their door: once the danger has passed, they slowly return to the old patterns, whether it be immediately or eventually.

Many of us do the very same thing when faced with painful situations.

PAIN AS THE CATALYST TO CHANGE

When you are awakened by pain, I think the universe, God, spirit, collective consciousness, a higher power—or whatever you choose to call it—is sending you a sign that you need to change. It is a warning flare that something is wrong.

This pain compelling you to change is the catalyst that allows you to find the path out of it. The path may be in the form of seeking guidance, knowledge, help, shifting your way of thinking (beliefs), or taking action to change your behavior.

If you can sustain the period of seeking long enough, and if you don't numb out or ignore the issue, the path forward will eventually become clear. It is a matter of trusting the unfolding process.

Sometimes the greater the pain, the greater the level of change is needed. This can be especially true if you have been suppressing, repressing, or ignoring the issue for a long time.

C.S. Lewis spoke of this very issue when he said, "God whispers to us in our pleasures, speaks in our consciences, but shouts in our pains. It is his megaphone to rouse a deaf world."

It doesn't matter what you believe about God. If you are experiencing pain, it can either be a point of transformation upward or a path down. It doesn't matter whether you call it the universe, life source, higher power, deity, or the divine!

The two questions to ask yourself are:

1. Have you gone deaf, dumb, or blind in some area of your life?
2. Is some-*one* or some-*thing* screaming out to get your attention?

Once you are crystal clear about the answers to those questions, you are ready to proceed. This means you have to decide whether you want this change to be permanent or temporary.

THE PATH TO CONSCIOUS CHANGE

This pain calling us toward change can be a tipping point forward or a blip on the radar screen of your life. You can use it as a catalyst for future changes you need to make, or you can fall back asleep, back to the old beliefs and the old ways.

The gift (opportunity) we receive from the pain of change materializes in your life when you leverage the awakening and use it as a springboard to carry you toward the next level of change. If we use it as a catalyst for future change, we end the pattern of sleepwalking our way through life and view it in a fully conscious, fully awake, and fully alive way.

We shift our mindset from waiting for the locus of change to be an external force and we shift to an internally-driven force, propelling us forward. We now embrace change, seeking new ways to go outside of what is common, known, and comfortable in all aspects of our lives. This is how we create and live an extraordinary life.

So how do you want to navigate through change? Do you want to bounce back and forth between being awake and asleep, staying awake just long enough to get relief from the current painful situation? Or do you want to embrace a mindset that gives you the energy and momentum to go to the next level where the change is calling you forward, pulling you toward purpose?

CHAPTER 8
THE 3RD LEVEL OF CHANGE – THE PULL (CALL)

The two most important days in life are the day you are born and the day you find out why.

Mark Twain

CONSCIOUS CHANGE AND YOUR PURPOSE

In every twelve-step program, they say the only step you have to get right is the first step, admitting you have a problem.

I think the same philosophy applies to the process of change. The first part of the change process that you need to get right is admitting you need to change. Once you do that, you can begin the real work of changing

In the twelve-step recovery process, the transformation accelerates greatly when you get to step four. There you start working on yourself and becoming conscious of the underlying issues causing the problem. These underlying issues operate at an unconscious level. The following steps bring these issues to the surface, so you can become conscious of them and then work to resolve them.

At the core of most addicts are ego and self-centeredness. For the record, I believe we are all addicts of something, whether it is being addicted to our thinking, our need to be right, to be in control, consumerism, binging television shows, social media, sweets, etc.. It doesn't matter what it is.

We all have attachments to things that help us hide from, run from, numb out, or avoid facing or feeling the effects of our problems. As I wrote in Chapters 4 and 5, it is our ego and our fear behind the wheel, steering the car that carries us off the road and into a ditch.

The ultimate goal of the twelve steps is to transform people into the best version of themselves. This is identical to the purpose behind being conscious and awake and seeing life as an opportunity to continuously move beyond your comfort zones toward living an extraordinary life.

At some point in the process, you realize that there is some force or energy drawing you forward. It is not pushing you, but it's calling you. It's drawing you to become the best version of your true self, and this is where you can live an extraordinary life!

REALIZING YOUR BRILLIANCE, GENIUS, AND CALLING

When we talk about brilliance, we are referring to the places where you truly shine. It is in these places where the facets reflect your genius outward to others.

Your genius (orig. genie) is where you find your magic. It includes the combination of your talents and strengths that is unique to you, even if you have an identical twin. It really doesn't have anything to do with your level of intelligence or I.Q.

Another way of framing this is to say that everyone has genius in them.

As Marianne Williamson so eloquently spoke in her frequently-referenced quote, "Words to Live By": "It is not just in some of us, it is in all of us!"[4] Your genius is the unique mix of talents, skills, strengths, and magic that only you can offer the world. To uncover it, you need to look inward and become conscious and aware of this unique offering.

Unfortunately, the world teaches us that we are what we wear, drive, eat, have in the bank, or project on social media. But that could not be farther from the truth. We are told to focus outwardly for our sense of self-worth and value. The truth is that all those things drive us away from our calling instead of toward it.

Your calling is the path where your genius and your brilliance combine to serve as a guide, a lighthouse, and a way to a greater purpose than you. It is how we find meaning in life. It is how we discover our true self.

This true self draws, pulls, and calls you home, where you become the very best version of yourself!

CALLING YOU HOME

It is said that a person realizes the greatest gift they can ever receive is when they give away their greatest gifts to serve others. This can be referred to as being enlightened, fully conscious or fully awake. This is how I define a purpose-driven life, a life free from the dogmatic, religious context that a purpose-driven life has sometimes been associated. In some ways it is analogous to the way "servant leadership" has been hijacked and rebranded as a form of being a good Christian leader. It is sooooooo much bigger than that!

If we are to make this leap and discover and live our purpose, we must experience and embrace our whole life, which includes the ups and downs, the good and not so good, the dark and the light, the joy and the sorrow, and the full spectrum.

Some avoid certain aspects of life and all it has to offer. They die, never having fully lived. Instead, they work extremely hard at filling their need to stay comfortable, safe, and within the walls of what is common, known, and safe. They are unaware that they are robbing themselves of the very life they are attempting to protect.

It was Henry David Thoreau who said, "When it comes time to die, let us not discover that we have never lived."

You cannot live an extraordinary life by hiding behind the walls of your comfort zone.

CHAPTER 9
SUSTAINING CHANGE

Be the Change You Wish to See in the World

Gandhi

There are consistently two challenges voiced in every organization I have ever engaged with in my business for nearly a quarter century. When I ask, "What is the biggest challenge facing your company?" I can guarantee practically ninety-nine-point-nine percent of the time, the answer will either be Communication or Change!

When people fail to examine their patterns of communication, they are basically saying they will not change. When they examine their communication issues and not do anything to change them, they are saying we will not change.

Our inability to not just change, but to sustain change, is at the core of all failing organizations. This is one of the key factors that keeps not just organizations from succeeding, but also most people.

This is why, when it comes to health club membership and New Years' Resolutions statistics, we find the following data:[5]

- On January 1, there is a 55% increase in gym attendance for

those aged 40 to 49, while a 65% increase was seen in the 50 to 59 age bracket.
- In an article published by the Hustle in 2019, they reported that 63% of memberships go completely unused and 82% of gym members go to the gym less than once per week.
- Moreover, 22% completely stop going six months into their membership, and 31% say they never would've paid had they known how little they'd use it.
- 50% of all new gym members quit going within six months of their annual membership.

While the Covid pandemic has certainly altered those numbers, the patterns remain the same.

People change and attempt to change all the time. For some reason, it is usually just a matter of time before they revert to the old habits.

We seem to do a much better job directing the change in others than we are at sustaining the change we desire in ourselves.

CHANGE WHO?

For so many years than I care to name, I have seen countless leaders, parents, teachers, and spouses attempting to change someone other than themselves.

We see this in marriages where people actually believe they can change their spouse after the wedding. Twenty years later they conclude that it was a waste of time. They either learn to accept the person, or they wade through hours of couple's therapy trying to find common-ground and a way to co-exist.

We see this in the workplace, where a leader sees so much more potential in one of their people than that person sees in themselves. They end up investing inordinate amounts of time trying to wake them up when the best they could do is cut them loose. During leadership development workshops, I've seen it hundreds of times, when leaders come to the awareness that they have been spending 80 percent of their time with the 20 percent of their people who are creating 80 percent of their problems because they are unwilling to change.

Leaders who believe their purpose is to save their people usually end up being the ones nailed to the tree.

To fully understand the concept of change, we need to embrace the idea that we can create an environment for people to grow and change, but we cannot change them! We are not responsible for their change.

This leads us to an essential truth: We are responsible and capable of only changing ourselves.

CHANGE WHAT?

I believe that the reason we fail to sustain the change we desire, is because we focus on changing the wrong thing.

These short-lived behavioral changes seem to change us for a time, but rarely is it long-term.

If you follow the diagram below, it states that our beliefs drive us to behave (act) in a certain way. Our behaviors (actions) then drive the results we are or are not achieving in life. The results we achieve just reaffirm our beliefs.

When we decide to make a change, it is usually the result of being unhappy with the result we are achieving. We then examine the cause of the results, which is the behavior. And while the behavior is causing us undesired results, it is not the root cause.

This is why we change for a time and then revert back to the old behavior. We must look deeper.

To sustain the change, you need to look at the underlying belief. We must look further to the underlying belief that drives the behavior. Otherwise, we never change at a deep level that is lasting or sustainable.

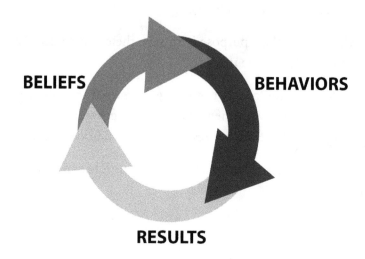

One of my many mentors, Dr. Nido Qubein, told me, "Joe, without the why, the how and the what don't matter!" Those words have stuck with me for years.

Most folks skip over the why and focus on the what and the how. I have always felt that without a clear understanding or purpose behind my actions, I was often distracted and slid off my path, no matter how good my intentions or how strong my effort, which leads me to my next point: If you are serious about changing and sustaining that change, you need to have clarity about why you want change. Without clarity it is next to impossible to focus. Without focus it is next to impossible to sustain the effort.

Below are three questions that could help you gain clarity on the *whyness* of changing so you don't flounder around in the how's and the what's.

Questions to clarify your purpose for changing:

1. How would your life be different and better if this change were unfolding in your life?
2. What happens if you don't change a thing? What is the cost?
3. Are you willing to accept the cost of not changing? If so, why? If not, why not?

Although simple, these questions help you gain clarity on what is driving the change. I find it beneficial to actually write down the answers and share them with someone who will listen, ask non-judgmental questions, and not give you an opinion or some advice, especially if you do not ask for it.

THE CANVAS

Very early in life, prior to being born, we were already impacted by external factors. Because our internal systems are delicately interwoven with our mothers, we experience many of the same emotional responses.

When a mother feels joy, her body releases dopamine and serotonin, two types of neurotransmitters in the brain associated with happiness. If a mother is frightened or lives with a mindset that the world is a hostile place, then her brain will tell the body to release adrenaline, cortisol, and epinephrine into the bloodstream.

Imagine these hormones swirling through her system and yours simultaneously.

Research has shown that fear and anxiety in the mother during pregnancy can negatively impact a young child in a number of ways: biologically, mentally, behaviorally, and medically.

Some of the effects show up in low height and birth weights, increased hyperactivity and lack of concentration, negative impacts on the child's growth and development of the nervous system, as well as endocrine disorders.[6]

Some of us may have very well been impacted by this experience in ways we might not realize until much later in life. As we gain insight into ourselves and deepen our levels of consciousness, we may see that we were being conditioned prior to even being born.

IMPRINTING

Once we are born, the external process of imprinting begins. Our parents, priests, rabbis, teachers, friends, relatives, and life experiences play a role in forming our internal belief systems.

For the first twelve to fourteen years, it is pretty much a direct download. Our initial beliefs about things like gender, race, religion, education, family, and success are formed during this time. Think of a plain white canvas being splashed with images that represent your beliefs. Once the canvas is filled, we go into the world and compare what is on our canvas to what we see and experience in the world.

Once we hit the adolescent stage of our development, we question some of our internal beliefs (the colors and images on our canvas) as we strive to find our own identity and separate from what we were taught. This can be a time of rebellion against authority and what is known.

If we are to evolve toward our purpose, we must be willing to realign, readjust, or completely dispose of some of the beliefs that we were imprinted with that no longer serve us. Some people find that their beliefs about things such as religion, relationships, and marriage are different from what their parents told or displayed for them and they no longer align or agree with the original imprinted belief. Others hold onto those original beliefs their entire lives. Neither way is right or wrong, unless you are not happy, or the results you are achieving are a far cry from what you truly want.

I coach a lot of people whose unconscious beliefs are giving them the exact opposite results of what they say they want. Coaching is a way to hold up a mirror so they can see themselves fully and awaken to this reality. It is then that a change can take place. But you must be open-minded in order to jettison some of those deeply embedded beliefs holding you back.

EMBEDDED BELIEFS

As human beings, we have evolved and been taught to see things in an either-or binary way. Early on, it was a way of keeping us alive. Thousands of years ago we had to make decisions in the context of safe and unsafe, eat or be eaten. We were fighting for survival. This type of thinking is referred to as dualistic and is a way to navigate the world. We will go into much greater detail later in this book. For now, it is important to understand that if we are to move beyond what is common, known, and safe, we must at times step back from this binary thinking and see a much bigger picture that expands our mindset. This allows us to hold both sides of an idea, situation, conflict, and the spectrum between the two end points without judging, condemning, or excluding.

To shift, transform, and change the results we are achieving, we must examine the underlying beliefs that drive us to act, which means we must be willing to flex, alter, or totally rewrite the underlying beliefs, especially if the results are not what we desire.

Our inner cumulative system of beliefs (our inner canvas) is what drives our actions and determines how we face problems, encounter challenges, and live life in general. This system creates our mindset. If you want to live an extraordinary life, you will need to change your mindset, which is what this chapter is all about. You must shift, alter, or reshape your beliefs.

EXERCISE TO REBELIEF

1. Select five key areas in your life that are important to you. (Relationships, Family, Finances, Success, Marriage, etc.)
2. Write them down on the left-hand side of a sheet of paper.
3. Without over-analyzing or over-thinking, write down what you

truly believe—the underlying belief you hold about that particular area of your life—on the left-hand side of the page.

4. On a scale from 1 to 10, with 1 being very low and 10 being extremely high, how would you rate the results you are achieving in that area of your life?
5. If you have been brutally honest, your results will correspond with the underlying belief.
6. Pick one area where you would like to achieve a different result. What is the number you want to achieve in that area of your life?
7. Ask yourself, "What is the underlying belief I need to have to achieve that desired result?" For example, if you examine your relationship with money, you will more than likely find the underlying and sometimes unconscious belief is the antithesis of what you really want. How must you change your belief to give you the results you truly want?

It is has been my experience that the results we achieve in life, especially when they are not what we want, have an umbilical cord that is directly tied to our self-worth and value. If we believe we don't deserve love, we will never achieve it. If we believe that we don't deserve to be financially successful, we never will be.

Like many things in life, shifting our beliefs is simple, but it is not easy. It is difficult to achieve, especially if we do not put a basic infrastructure in place to guide our efforts.

Now that you have done the foundational work, you need to put the change into a system—an infrastructure—to sustain it.

CHAPTER 10
HOW DO I CHANGE? – DISCIPLINE & CONSISTENCY

We must all suffer one of two things: the pain of discipline or the pain of regret or disappointment.

Jim Rohn

DISCIPLINE & CONSISTENCY – NO THANK YOU!

I have spent nearly four decades in the business world, and more than twenty of those years were spent coaching leaders, yet I am consistently surprised that most people fail to comprehend that they hold within themselves the power to change. They also lack the discipline to consistently sustain the change.

Most recently, I was working with a group of leaders who had experienced fairly negative results from an organizational employee survey. During the program to reshape the culture (I define culture as the collective beliefs and behaviors of the group), one of the values they chose to act upon was sustaining the change. In other words, they chose discipline and consistency.

What I found most interesting was they all spoke of similar sessions in the past where everyone walked out feeling great, and within three to four weeks, they fell back into their old patterns as if nothing ever happened. Corporate then sent another well-intentioned initiative down the corporate ladder, and they moved onto the next initiative du jour, usually because someone in the ivory tower met a guy like me on a plane or read a fascinating new book!

The same scenario unfolds in the life of individuals. We attempt to change, we change for a bit, and then we fall back as a result of no discipline or consistency. Think about how many times you've attempted to change some aspect of your life only to find yourself revisiting the very same issue a week or a month later, even if and when we see improvement or a good result.

THE ILLUSION OF FREEDOM

Growing up in the 1970s in an Italian family, it was not uncommon to hear Frank Sinatra belting out his version of "I Did it My Way," on the phonograph—yes, the phonograph!

I believe there is an inherent conviction in most folks that discipline and consistency are restrictions of their freedom—someone stepping on their individual rights—and this is a predominant belief in the American Culture. As wonderful and free as it sounds, it is a false narrative.

I recently experienced this while the world experienced the Covid-19 pandemic. Over the course of a relatively short period of time, I found myself slowly being lulled to sleep and falling into old patterns again!

Throughout the first three months or so of the pandemic, as restaurants, gyms, bars, and stores were being shut down, I found myself with an excess amount of time based on a few other decisions I had made. I also experienced a magnified sense of freedom, even though my choices were somewhat limited. I slowly began to fill my time increasing my food and alcohol intake, along with my intake of social and broadcast media, as I looked for ways to fill the space.

One day, I woke up with a sense of urgency that I was wasting my life and precious amounts of time, allowing external factors to negatively impact the results I was achieving. While I realized a pandemic was skyrocketing out of control around me, I also realized that I still had the power of choice regarding how I spent my time and what I allowed to impact my mindset.

Freedom comes from choosing how to spend your time and being in control of what you allow to impact your thinking. Some people fear discipline and consistency in their life for fear of losing their freedom, but discipline and consistency provide even more freedom.

TRULY FREE TO CHOOSE

To reverse the effect I had allowed the pandemic to have on my life, I realized that I first needed to be reminded of my life's purpose (my why) and my values (what was important), and then realign those with the actions (how's and what's) I needed to take. First refocus on your why, then on what is important, and finally work to understand the how and the what!

I then sat down and reflected on the previous year, realizing I had achieved my three-year business goals to write another book, develop a leadership development program, had the most successful year financially in twenty years, and achieved financial freedom.

Even though I had business goals for the current year, I realized they needed to be recalibrated to adjust for the impact the pandemic had on my business.

I also reevaluated another area of my life I had been putting off for years—my relationships.

I had had a string of unsuccessful relationships and two failed marriages.

CHAPTER 10

When I looked back at the trail of carnage, I realized that the cause, the constant, and the dis-ease was me. I had left my fingerprints all over the scene of every crime.

This is a different process for people in their mid-to-late 50s versus their 30s or 40s. The trail is usually longer, and the window of opportunity in front of them is no longer a giant floor to ceiling, wall-to-wall picture window. The long view of life was shortening and there was a magnified sense of urgency that time was running out. It was a heavy realization.

Although I have had many successes in my life, for some reason, this was different. I think the pandemic altered everyone's reality, especially mine, and it sent a huge wake-up tremor throughout the world for a lot of folks.

I wanted to end the roller coaster of ups and downs knowing that I wanted to finish this life on the highest note possible. I wanted to be able to say that I had truly lived an extraordinary life.

Once I recalibrated, realigned, and created a plan, I came to the realization that I wanted to ensure that the plan, which kept me disciplined and consistent, would also have some form of built-in accountability.

I knew I needed accountability, and I knew exactly where to find it!

CHAPTER 11
HOW DO I CHANGE? – THE A-WORD

Accountability is a word that we hear a lot. As often as we hear it, you would think most folks would have found a way to overcome the lack of accountability in their lives, yet they haven't.

Like discipline and consistency, I believe that most people believe that accountability is an impingement on their freedom. Having someone else in our lives to make sure we do what we say we will do seems childish, but I have found that without accountability, my ability to account for my results is weakened immensely.

When I finally woke up, I had to own that I had been lacking the discipline and consistency I needed to get back on track. I knew the next step was finding someone or something to be accountable to other than myself.

I realized that the most productive times in my life and my career were when I had been part of a daily call at 5:15 a.m., which was developed by my friend and colleague, Shawna Schuh.

During this time, my business was on fire, my coaching business was filled, I had created a seven-month leadership development program and was delivering it to companies across the U.S., we had redesigned the new website, and I was putting the finishing touches on my third book.

So what happened? I dropped off the call and decided to go my own way for a while.

Like most things that are good for you, when you stop, you don't feel the results immediately. You feel them eventually. Eating one donut is not going to send you to the ER, especially if you normally take care of yourself, but eating one donut three times a day for a year just might.

The momentum from being on the call for years allowed me to continue at a fairly high level. In fact, it carried me all the way till the end of 2019, when I successfully completed the best year I have ever had in business.

By the end of May 2020, the pandemic was spreading like a wildfire throughout the world. After navigating through my first three months of isolation and quarantining, I found myself feeling empty, off-course, lacking discipline and consistency, and in dire need of accountability. In other words, I was failing!

YOU CANNOT DO IT ALONE

Coming to the realization and owning the truth that I was failing required swallowing a large dose of humility. No matter how you rationalize it, humility, like limburger cheese, tastes horrible. I think most of us believe that to lean on others for our success is a sign of weakness. The truth is we cannot do it alone!

Even though I had already shifted my mindset and set up the infrastructure for consistency, I still needed the last piece of the puzzle. I got back on the 5:15 a.m. call and started being held accountable for my commitments in a small community of like-minded folks. Just like that, my productivity sky-rocketed! I started writing another book—this one in fact—and my client list was growing, even while the pandemic was ramping up full-force.

I came back to the realization that I had even more freedom than I had before. Freedom without the guilt of feeling like an unproductive, unmotivated putz. There was more flexibility in my schedule because I was starting my day at 5:00 a.m. If I wanted to, I could end my day at 2 p.m. or 3 p.m. without the guilt. Why? Because I had worked for nine to ten hours. If I wanted to keep working, I did!

So what about you? What in this chapter resonates for you? What is the one idea or action you know you need to take? Where are you lacking the discipline and consistency, and where will you go to get accountable? Not sure?

As we close out this portion of the book, I think this is a great time to ask yourself how committed you are in creating and living the extraordinary life you say you want. I believe you. Do you believe you?

Below is a list of questions to embed the thoughts, desires, beliefs, and actions into your neuropaths.

TEN QUESTIONS YOU NEED TO ANSWER BEFORE YOU COMMIT TO CHANGE

1. Are you satisfied with the level of success, love, happiness, and joy that you have in your life? If yes, stop here!
2. What's missing from your life, or in what area do you want or need something more or different?
3. In what way is that missing component negatively impacting your life?
4. How does not having it or clinging to it actually serve you? In other words what do you get from not pursuing it? Your answer can be things like no responsibility, no pressure, perceived freedom, etc.
5. How would your life be different if you had it? Be detailed here.
6. What would you be willing to give up in order to achieve it? Are you sure?

7. What happens if you don't change a thing? Are you okay with that?
8. What underlying belief is creating the misalignment with the results you want to achieve? Are you willing to let it go? Revisit question 4 and ask yourself if that is what you really want. If it is, that's okay. It is better to be honest than to keep beating the hell out of yourself for not achieving something you really don't want.
9. Who could be your accountability partner in this process? This is important as you need someone who can balance the spectrum of kicking your butt and loving encouragement when you are struggling.
10. What would be the next three steps to take to get this process started?

Are you ready to start crafting your extraordinary life?

THE EXTRAORDINARY YOU

The world will tell you that you are not enough of one thing and too much of another. You will hear all sorts of negative messages from parents, teachers, peers, clergy, bosses, friends, spouses, partners, and the most insidious of them all, institutions like the government, some religious organizations, and the media—both broadcast and social.

These messages will tell you that you cannot do or be X or Y. Some of them will even tell you why you cannot. The reasons may at times be logical, and at other times, they will absolutely defy any rational reason.

And yet…

If you want to live a life that is extraordinary you must cast aside what other people tell you is right for you and decide for yourself what is right, or extraordinary for you. As I mentioned before, extraordinary is different for every individual on this earth. No one can decide what is extraordinary for you. An often-used quote originating in the bible and echoed by JFK states, "to whom much is given, much is required."

Required by whom? Of Self or of Another? Perhaps it's required by your parents, your spouse, your kids, or your boss?

Why do you choose to do what you do? Is it to please others or is it to become the best version of yourself? It happens thousands of times a day all over the world. There is the spouse who chooses to stay married for the sake of the kids and lives a life of emptiness with a dull but constant ache in their heart, and for what? So they can teach their children how not to do a marriage?

Then there is the child who dreams of being an actor, but instead joins the family business because that is what is expected, and spends the rest of life trying to fill the hole with bigger and bigger toys.

CHAPTER 11

What about addicts who decide to get clean and sober to please someone else and not because they have hit bottom or don't want to live that way any longer. They then constantly slip in and out of using.

Doing something because someone else wants you to and not to become the best version of yourself can result in a life of selling yourself out.

I wanted to share a story about successful people who never gave up on their dreams, as such Mark Cuban, Harrison Ford, Suze Orman, J.K. Rowling, Ang Lee, Mary Kay Ash, or Ray Kroc.

But then we would simply be projecting on to them our belief that they had extraordinary lives, based on what we saw and not what we knew. Should we measure an extraordinary life based on financial success or notoriety, or should we measure it based on what we believe deep down in the core of our souls?

Living your extraordinary life means you must be crystal clear about what "extraordinary" is for you at the core of your soul. An extraordinary life isn't defined by one giant leap, although it could be. More than likely, your extraordinary life will be comprised of all the small incremental choices you make, inching you forward every time you go outside your comfort zone.

1. So what does your extraordinary look like for you?
2. What is one area of your life that could be even more extraordinary? Extraordinary Love, and is it Love of Self, Love of Another, etc.
3. Is there anything stopping or blocking you from going outside of your comfort zone in that one area of your life?

As a coach once said to me about a similar situation, cut out that crap!

Now let us start looking at the facets of your life so you can start transforming the rock that will ground you in the life that you choose.

My wish is that you choose a life that is, well, *extraordinary*!

PART II
BEING EXTRAORDINARY

Part I was all about setting up the framework and creating the foundation to build an extraordinary life. At this point, we need to look at the various areas of your life so you can define for yourself what being extraordinary would be for you, knowing that extraordinary is a very personal thing.

You can compare yourself, your career, your kids, your family, your partner, or your spouse to everyone else's if you would like to, but someone once said that when you compare yourself to someone else, only two things can happen. Neither one of them is good. You raise yourself above them to feel better about yourself, albeit temporary, or you lower yourself to be below or behind them and then feel miserable about yourself.

The beautiful, magnificent thing about being extraordinary is that your version of extraordinary is unique to you. As long as you are moving outside of your comfort zones, or going "outside" of what you know, you cannot help but live life in an extraordinary way.

CHAPTER 12
HOW LONG DOES IT TAKE TO BECOME EXTRAORDINARY?

How long does it take you, as boss, to achieve world-class quality? Less than a nanosecond to attain it, a lifetime of passionate pursuit to maintain it.

Tom Peters, *The Pursuit of Wow!*

A NANOSECOND

When best-selling author and business guru, Tom Peters, addressed the issue of how long it would take to become world-class, he simply stated, "Less than a nanosecond to be it..."

I believe that being extraordinary is no different from being world-class. It takes less than a nanosecond to be it. You just have to decide.

And while that sounds simple (because it is), our brains want to make it more complex. Maybe this is a way the ego steps in and helps us to avoid embracing our inner brilliance? Maybe we fear being extraordinary?

Either way, you simply must decide. Remember that not deciding is itself a decision.

DECIDING TO BE EXTRAORDINARY

When you decide to live an extraordinary life, the next step is examining all the various facets of our lives, reflecting on what areas are working and which might need some cutting or reshaping because they are not reflecting the life we want to live or lead.

It's like what happens when a diamond cutter first examines an uncut stone. Most diamond cutters first study the stone and then decide on a plan to determine what needs to be removed and what must be left in place. The idea is to bring out the unique brilliance of that particular stone.

Just like every diamond is unique to itself, so is every human being, which means that the plan and blueprint for an extraordinary life for everyone is as unique as every diamond.

You need to examine yourself, putting together a plan by deciding what stays and what goes in order for you to shine in your utmost brilliance.

STAYING EXTRAORDINARY

The first half of Tom Peters's quote addresses how long it takes to attain world-class success, happiness, or whatever goal you wish to choose. The second half of his quote was what he added, which brought the reality of being world-class into a person's life when he said, "and a lifetime to maintain it."

So it reads, "Less than a nanosecond to be it and a lifetime to maintain it."

This is very similar to the decision to change! Just because you contemplate change or changing doesn't mean you have changed. The real work of change comes from lifelong execution to maintain it.

Similarly, just because you've decided to be extraordinary, it doesn't mean you are. The real work is in the lifelong commitment and execution to stay extraordinary, which is why we spent pretty much the first part of this book analyzing, dissecting, and discussing change. Change is the capstone that drives everything else in life, which is why discipline, consistency and accountability are so critical to insuring we continue the process of living an extraordinary life.

NOT FOR THE WEAK OF...

There is a saying when something is difficult or challenging: "It is not for the weak of heart." I think deciding to live an extraordinary life is not for the weak of heart, mind, soul, or anything else you want to tack on to the list!

It is an incredibly daunting process! Why? Because as you push yourself to expand beyond what is comfortable, it changes in two ways. First, each push moves you to a new and different level of uncomfortableness. Second, the life force that drives you to change (Chapter 6 – The Push) shifts as you age. What was uncomfortable at the age of twenty is much different from what is uncomfortable at the age of forty, sixty, or even ninety.

What was physically easy at twenty or forty has been altered by the time you reach sixty or seventy, so you must shift your approach. That is why it is so important to make sure you are seeing things clearly.

CHAPTER 13
EXTRAORDINARY VISION

*If the doors of **perception** were cleansed,*

everything would appear to man as it is, infinite.

For man has closed himself up,

till he sees all things through narrow chinks of his cavern.

William Blake

How you see the world is impacted greatly by your thoughts and underlying beliefs. Our beliefs color the lenses we use to see the world. Our perception includes many different lenses, which include but are not limited to gender, education, family-of-origin, race, religion, culture, life experiences, etc.

Some of us struggle with seeing clearly with our eyesight because of either nearsightedness, farsightedness, or astigmatisms. These types of impairments can also affect the way we see the world and those around us.

In the world of optometry, if you have problems with your vision, the most common issues are:

- Nearsighted: the inability to see things clearly that are far away

- Farsighted: the inability to see things clearly that are close
- Astigmatism: a blurred area within an otherwise clear image - basically a blind spot

If you are suffering from one of these issues, your optometrist will prescribe lenses so your vision can be corrected. The same principals apply to your perception of the world and others. Perception is derived from its root word, "perceive," which literally means "to take," as in "to take in." When we perceive something, we take it in through our lenses and then attempt to make sense of it as we filter it through our lenses (belief system).

We discussed in Chapter 9 the importance of shifting or expanding our beliefs because they have a direct correlation to the results we are achieving in any given area of our life, but what happens when our vision is off? What happens when we fail to see things up close, or far away, or whether we are unaware of a blind spot that prevents us from seeing things as William Blake described—"infinite?" What if we are interpreting the world and everything in it from a narrow slit in the window (dualistic thinking)?

Living an extraordinary life requires that we have the correct vision to see both near and far, without the blind spots keeping us from seeing the things we need to change for us to grow. If your vision is not clear, you may find yourself constantly bumping into things. After a while that can be both painful and frustrating, especially if they are the same obstacles getting in our way again and again!

THREE THINGS THAT CAN AFFECT YOUR VISION AND WHAT YOU CAN DO ABOUT IT

Nearsightedness: Folks who are nearsighted tend to get stuck in old patterns and old ways of thinking. They can only see things as they are and struggle to think outside the box. We refer to this as being short-sighted or an inability to see the forest from the trees. These people tend to think small and less futuristic. They may hold their cards close to the vest and might lean toward the risk-adverse side of things.

They can really struggle with the idea of being extraordinary because they are unable to push beyond their comfort zones and what they've always known or done. Their vision won't allow them to. If this is where you are, you need to involve others you trust in on what you want. You have to have folks who will push you and hold you accountable. You need people who can pick you up and dust you off when you fail, give you a pat on the ass, and send you back in the game. Coaches can be excellent tools to help you here because they are usually people you do not know, and since they have no emotional skin in the game, they can be brutally honest.

Farsightedness: Folks who are farsighted tend to gloss over the details. They can overlook the "real" issues and may end up treating the symptoms instead of the dis-ease. They tend to think big and conceptually. This think-big mindset can keep them from having a concrete plan or paying attention to the details, so sometimes the details may fall through the cracks.

They may think out loud, so they can ramble on as they verbally work through an idea. They may not always be the best planner, as it is easy for them to get distracted from the mission. They may need to slow down and identify the real underlying issues (the devil) that can be found in the details.

It is important that they surround themselves with accountability partners who can bring them back down to earth. These big thinkers can get bored quickly with the more mundane tasks and will move on to the next new big idea before they finish what they have started. That is why again, it is so important to understand what type of accountability partner is best for you.

Astigmatisms: Everyone has some type of astigmatism when it comes to how we see the world. While being nearsighted or farsighted is more general in nature, an astigmatism can be very specific and very personal. One of the biggest blind spots that impacts our vison the greatest is our ego, which we discussed at length in Chapter 4. The second biggest astigmatism preventing most people from seeing clearly is a dualistic mindset where we see everything as black and white. I am not saying there are not times when we need to see things as black and white, for instance when wiring a home for electricity, but when it comes to people and complex issues, dualistic thinking can be very detrimental.

When we see the world through our own lenses and feel we must put the person, place, thing, or situation in the right or wrong, good or bad, or the safe or unsafe pile, we become critical, judgmental, and closed-minded. We are blind and cannot see the big picture. When we cannot or choose not to see the whole picture, we stay stuck, stay common, and never go 'outside' our ability to live an extraordinary life.

With all things, it is critical to have people in your life who tell you what you need to hear, even when you don't want to hear it, instead of simply being surrounded with folks who tell you what you want to hear.

A mentor of mine once said that if one person calls you a horse's ass, blow it off. If two people tell you you're a horse's ass, you might want to pay attention. However, if three people tell you you're a horse's ass, buy a saddle!

Ask your accountability partner or the five people you spend the most time with the following three questions. It just might give you some insight into any astigmatisms that are holding you back.

1. What works about me as a _____ (partner, spouse, father, friend, etc.)?
2. Is there anything that doesn't?
3. What is the one thing I could do that would have the single most positive impact on our relationship, business, family, friendship, etc.?

Write down what they say. Don't respond or defend. Simply say, "Thank you."

CHAPTER 14
EXTRAORDINARY HUMILITY

EXPLORING EXTRAORDINARY HUMILITY

We discussed humility in the latter part of Chapter 5, in the context of reducing the ego. We said that to eliminate ego, you need to have a sense of humility and acceptance. We also mentioned that most folks struggle with the difference between being humble and being humiliated.

Now might be a good touchstone to define what extraordinary humility looks like.

EXTRAORDINARY HUMILITY IS...

We discussed earlier that the ability to experience extraordinary humility requires a dissolving of the ego. If you make everything about you and are easily offended by the actions of others, then you are on the wrong side of the humility versus humiliation equation. If you fail in your ability to tame your ego, you may end up making a fool of yourself even though you may make some good decisions.

Donald Trump was a great example of this concept. Regardless of your politics, whether you are pro or against, he represents the embodiment of someone who lacks humility. As president of the United States, you would expect he would have a certain level of confidence. After all, he was the president. But he didn't. What his bravado represented was an inner insecurity. His insecurity was so big that he felt he had to constantly inflate himself on a daily or even hourly basis, thus the constant tweeting.

If anyone, the president of the United States should carry a certain level of impenetrable confidence. Having an innate confidence in who I am should come with a certain level of humility, especially if I know that my sense of self-worth and value is an internal value or character I hold.

Based on the behaviors Trump had displayed, it was quite easy to see that regardless of what he said, his actions reflected an inner sense of self-worth and value that was almost non-existent, regardless of how many tweets or public pats on the back he gives himself.

It is basic, textbook psychology.

MONEY CAN'T BUY YOU LOVE OR SELF-WORTH

I believe when we reflect on Trump's presidency, we will see that money doesn't buy you love or self-worth and value, no matter how much you have. History shows us that folks who let go of the ego or false self, as it is sometimes referred, exhibit a level of confidence in knowing who they are. It isn't wrapped up in a false image or an incessant need to be right, to win, to be liked, or constantly seen, recognized, and/or adored.

The idea that humility is achieved through a dissolving of the ego is nothing new. It has been taught and preached about for thousands of years by much wiser folks than me. Dissolving the ego doesn't happen overnight. It will be a lifelong process filled with a few steps forward as well as a few steps back. The thing to remember is that as long as you are progressing forward, you are winning the battle for humility and the war of the ego.

It is a giant shift from living in your head to living out of your heart. It a transformation of your mindset that foundationally shakes where your heart stands.

TWELVE SIGNS YOU ARE MOVING TOWARD A HEART-BASED HUMILITY

1. Someone with diametrically-opposed political views attempts to push you into a conversation, and you reply with, "I guess I just don't know" or "I appreciate your thoughts. Thanks for sharing."
2. A person cuts you off on the freeway and you remain calm and think, *They must be in a hurry or are having a bad day.*
3. You hear a story about a group of folks whom you have at times been extremely judgmental about and you feel some sense of empathy toward them. Why? Because you realize we all have blind spots or areas we don't see.
4. You can be in a room with anyone and not get triggered by their actions or their words.
5. Someone in a meeting or social event is acting in an extremely arrogant (prideful, victim, etc.) manner, and you realize that your desire to judge them is really about you not wanting to own your own arrogance (pride, victimhood, etc.).
6. When another person is acting ignorantly or in an unkind way, you realize that you are not perfect either, at times struggle with your own challenges, so you let it go.
7. You're on the phone with your ninety-one-year-old Italian mother and she is telling you a story for the third time. Instead of getting angry, you think, *Someday, she won't be here to tell me another story.* You smile and listen anyway.
8. You're in a room full of people who are railing against a particular religious group, race, or gender, and you bow out of the conversation because you don't have to win or be right.
9. You understand that no matter what other people do or say, even if it is directed toward you, it has absolutely nothing to do with you.
10. You've given up the need to be right, make others feel lesser than,

or the need to win in an attempt to feel a false sense of self-worth or value.

11. You believe and embrace the idea that you are not responsible for changing anyone's thoughts, beliefs, or personality other than your own.
12. You know that individuals are on their own path and exactly where they are supposed to be, so you give them grace and accept them wherever they are at this moment in time.

Of course, you may slip back at times and exhibit the antithesis of these behaviors. That said, the most important thing to remember is as long as your overall progress is steadily moving forward, you are progressing. That's what counts!

Making progress in this way, extraordinary humility is adding to the many ways to live an extraordinary life. Eventually, you will realize that you cannot live an extraordinary life without giving and receiving extraordinary love.

CHAPTER 15
EXTRAORDINARY LOVE

Question: Why I am devoting three chapters to the topic of love?

Answer: Easy answer, you cannot live an extraordinary life without also experiencing extraordinary love.

Question: What makes you think you have the credibility to write about love?

Answer: I am not sure what makes one person more qualified than another to write about such an incredibly complex topic. I do know there are self-proclaimed experts who write about things they have never experienced. For example, I know of self-proclaimed leadership speakers and coaches who have never led anyone, teaching leadership skills to others.

Over the course of my lifetime, I have experienced many different types and intensity levels of love. I am by no means an expert on love. I really don't know who is. My goal here is to share my experience and thoughts on this extremely complicated topic. I realize these are my experiences and my thoughts. That doesn't make them yours. However, if you can glean even a small nugget of self-awareness or knowledge from what I share, then I have succeeded in my goal. As always, take what you like and leave the rest.

CHAPTER 15

LOVE IS COMPLEX

One of my favorite movies is the 1987 movie entitled *Moonstruck*, starring Cher as the young, widowed Loretta Castorini, along with a whole host of great actors. Maybe it is because I grew up in an Italian family that this movie hits home for me in so many ways. It encapsulates the craziness of love and family in a poignant but humorous way.

Loretta is engaged to Johnny Cammareri (Danny Aiello) who visits his sick dying mother in Sicily. While he's gone, she meets Johnny's brother Ronny Cammareri (Nicolas Cage), in an attempt to resolve bad blood between brothers. Instead of resolving the issues, she and Ronny fall in love.

One of the greatest scenes happens toward the end of the movie. It's breakfast time in the Castorini kitchen and the whole family including the in-laws are there. Johnny has just returned from visiting his dying mother, who had a miraculous recovery and got out of bed to start cooking for twenty-five people when she was told that her son was getting married.

This is a brilliantly-written script with impeccable timing. In a matter of minutes, Loretta's mother Rose (Olympia Dukakis) confronts her husband about issues in their marriage and they reaffirm their longtime love for each other. Loretta goes from being promised to one brother to being engaged to the other. The brothers make peace more or less. The weeping grandfather who is utterly confused recovers and welcomes Johnny into his brother's new family!

The classic line in the movie is when Rose asks Loretta if she loves Ronnie, saying, "Do you love him, Loretta?"

Loretta says, "Aw, Ma, I love him awful!"

Rose then responds by saying, "Oh God, that's too bad!"

In this short movie clip, the complexities and intricacies of love (all types of love) are woven in, out, around, and through the scene.

The point: there are many types of love, and they all have varying degrees of complexity in them.

WHAT'S LOVE GOT TO DO WITH IT? IS IT LOVE THAT I'M FEELING?

Love is not a black-and-white subject. It isn't a yes-or-no response, even though we might like to believe so. If it were that simple, people would not struggle with it as often and as much as they do.

Attempting to understand love is like trying to understand God, infinity, death, or the universe. You will never understand any of these topics by applying a dualistic mindset of good or bad, right or wrong, or any other either-or binary thought process.

Did you know that at one point in history, there were anywhere from five to eight different types of love or ways to describe the various forms of love between people and things. There were different words for all the different types of love.[7]

They were:

- *Agape* — empathetic, universal, unconditional love for everyone and everything
- *Eros* — romantic and passionate love. It includes personal adoration of another, pleasure, and desire
- *Philia* — intimate, authentic friendship and love without romantic attraction (friends and sometimes family)
- *Philautia* — self-love and compassion for oneself, which includes self-respect and self-acceptance
- *Storgē* — familiar, familial love. Love between parents and children or childhood friends
- *Pragma* — committed companion; a mature enduring love that develops over time

- *Ludus* — playful love and flirting, which is usually most evident in the beginning of an intimate relationship
- Mania — obsessive and jealous, or a madness. Unfortunately, it is more cathexis than actual love

Nowadays, there is basically one love.

I LOVE YOU AND MY CAR

For centuries, since the Age of Enlightenment, we leveraged words to describe events in more detail so we can understand or give things meaning. When it comes to one of the most important words in the human vocabulary, a word that has been described as the salve for the world, we have watered it down to basically one meaning, namely a strong, emotional feeling or intensity.

In our search as a race to label, define, describe, and make sense of love, we have diluted it down to an almost meaningless description of any and all intense emotional feelings or affections. "I love my wife" is as common as "I love my car." I love my job, my house, my kid, the Rolling Stones, Madonna, Rap Music, and the Cleveland Browns.

If I say I love my car, is that the same as loving my kid or my spouse? Of course not! However, I think we have simplified the word love down to a point where it isn't as meaningful as it once was.

So what is the true meaning of the word love? What does extraordinary love actually mean?

This search to understand love led me here.

EXTRAORDINARY DEFINITION OF LOVE

More than twenty-five years ago I read a book by psychologist and author M. Scott Peck. The book was entitled, *The Road Less Traveled*. It was originally published in 1978. It was an incredibly successful work and was on the frontier of modern-day psychotherapy. I guess when you sell over six million copies of a book world-wide, it must be good.

Peck's book contains what I believe is the finest definition of love I have ever read. Obviously, it is in the context of a relationship with living things and not your car, although some people might believe driving a particular car could be spiritual.

He defines love as:

> "The will to extend oneself for the purpose of nurturing one's own or another's spiritual growth."

It isn't flowery or romantic in any way; however, I believe it goes far beyond flowers, chocolates, and compatibility assessments from *Cosmopolitan Magazine*.

We have become a society of simple, easy, and fast. So much so that we see examples of people who treasure their possessions far more than their partner or their kids. We have watered down the word love to a point to where it stinks of codependency and possession far more than it speaks to a spiritual experience.

OUTSIDE OF YOURSELF

Putting oneself out there to grow isn't about religion, it is about who you are at your core. It is what the great spiritual teachers have spoken of when they speak about the soul.

Growing and developing as a human being doesn't mean that we go outside of ourselves to collect more possessions to be more comfortable or attempt to feel better about ourselves. Going outside of ourselves in the context of love is about going beyond our comfort zones and being uncomfortable. It is about breaking new ground or learning new things about ourselves and each other.

That, my friend, will always take you on a journey that is at times uncer-

CHAPTER 15

tain and unknown. At times you will feel scared, angry, lost, and not in control. It starts when you decide to love yourself and extend yourself for the purpose of nurturing your own spiritual growth.

You cannot love others if you do not love yourself. Call it cliché, call it simple, or call it what you will. However, there is nothing closer to the truth than the following simple saying, and this has been proven over and over again.

It starts with you!

CHAPTER 16
EXTRAORDINARY LOVE – SELF

If you don't love yourself, nobody will. Not only that, you won't be good at loving anyone else. Loving starts with the self.

Wayne Dyer

CHILDREN AND LOVE

I was never taught as a child to place love of myself before love of others. In fact, I was taught that love and acceptance of others was much higher on the priority list than me. A famous saying around our house was, "What would the neighbors say?"

Unfortunate events that took place around our house became a national publicized billboard for who we were as children and our reputation in the neighborhood. If I helped myself to two donuts at once, I was taught to believe that the following conversation could unfold between myself and the neighbor.

Neighbor: Joe, we were really looking forward to inviting you over to play with your friends! However, once we heard that you took two donuts from the box before the others had a chance to choose one, well, we decided you weren't the kind of kid we wanted hanging out and influencing our daughter Jeannie!"

Me: You're right Mrs. Gedeon. I was being bad. I am sorry I hurt you. It won't happen again. It is just that I am only five years old. I am supposed to be selfish and self-centered! Oh and one more thing, please don't think poorly of my mother, she is an amazing mom regardless of my behaviors. What I did has nothing to do with her or her parenting!"

WHAT OTHERS THINK

In his book *The Four Agreements,* author Don Miguel Ruiz refers to the process of raising children as the "domestication of humans." He speaks to the fact that how and what we teach our children is more about training them to conform to our mores, standards, and beliefs.

Many of us were taught to hold the love and acceptance of others in a much higher regard than the love and acceptance we have for ourselves.

Apparently, teaching children to obey and follow the rules is far more important than teaching them what it means to have self-worth and value that comes from within. We learn early on in life to please others and vie for their love and attention. We do this by being smart, pretty, successful, a good-boy or a good-girl, and or putting the needs of everyone else above our own, even if that means doing harm to ourselves.

We do this to children for a variety of reasons:

- So we can control them.
- Because we believe how the world perceives our children is how they see us as parents. Is my kid a good Christian? Smart? Talented? Then I must be as well, or I must be a great parent.
- We fear our children will become self-centered, selfish, narcissistic and believe everything is all about them. Well guess what? That experiment failed!
- We taught them a lie that they can control external factors that

they actually have no control over, and those external factors determine their self-worth and value.
- What others think about them and their self-image is dependent on what they do, how they look, how many followers they have on Instagram, what car they drive, or which version of the latest iPhone they possess.

To say we have fallen short would be a gross understatement!

IT ALL BEGINS WITH...

When we refer to loving oneself, we need to make sure we are not speaking about selfish, self-centered, narcissistic self-admiration. We are referring to loving yourself for who you are (authentically and genuinely), and it has nothing to do with what you own, where you live, or how you look. It has everything to do with who you are at your core without the masks and the facades.

Loving oneself means that we work and develop ourselves to be the best version of ourselves in every aspect of our lives—physically, mentally, emotionally, and spiritually (whatever that is for you).

I was speaking with a friend who was going through a tough break up. He talked about all of the hard work he had done to be a great partner, which felt like such a waste of time to him because the relationship ended anyway. I had to stop and ask him, "So are you doing the work on yourself to be the best partner for someone else, or are you doing it to be the best version of yourself for you?"

To me, changing for someone else is the equivalent of addicts getting sober to save their marriages, instead of getting sober because it is what they need to do for themselves. As soon as something goes wrong in the relationship, they back pedal and use again. This is why you need to work on becoming the best version of yourself, separate and disconnected from the umbilical cord that keeps you tethered to others. This is not an unproven hypothesis. It is a universal law—you cannot give away something you do not possess. Attempting to go around, over, under, in order to avoid a problem or circumvent a natural law usually ends in some type of natural disaster.

WHAT LOVING YOURSELF LOOKS LIKE

What might loving yourself possibly look like? While this is not an all-inclusive list, these questions may help you gain insight into healthy self-love.

Whether you answer with a yes or no isn't as important as answering them honestly.

Be brutally honest. You don't want to cheat yourself out of the experience or end up having this issue rear its ugly head in another part of your life.

1. Am I content with myself, regardless of whether I am in a significant relationship or alone?
2. Do I understand the difference between healthy boundaries and walls?
3. Do I consistently choose healthy boundaries?
4. Do I have hobbies, friends, and goals separate from my primary relationship?
5. Do I take 100 percent of the responsibility for the mistakes I have made in my past relationships?
6. Have I done the necessary work to be sure I am not repeating the same mistakes in my relationships/friendships over and over again?
7. Am I aware of how my upbringing has impacted my current relationships in both a positive and a not-so-positive way?
8. Do I continue to develop my sense of being mentally, spiritually, and emotionally balanced and healthy?
9. Am I free from addictions?
10. Do I continue to work toward being the best version of myself

because it is what I need to do for me, not my partner or a future partner?
11. Can I honestly say that I love myself?
12. Do I care for myself physically by getting enough rest, exercise, and am I conscience about how I treat my-self?
13. Relationally (choose one depending on where you are at this point in your life regarding a primary love relationship):
    a. Do I believe that when I am ready, I will attract the right partner for a relationship?
    b. Have I attracted the perfect partner who creates opportunities for me to work through my relationship issues?
    c. Do I have healthy boundaries and know whether to stay or exit a relationship I am in or considering?
14. Do I have a written list of values (non-negotiables) that guide the choices I make in life?
15. Am I clear about my purpose (why I am here) and do I consistently work toward achieving it?
16. Do I have a number of healthy relationships in my life that are very fulfilling?
17. Do I have a few very close friends in my life whom I trust and who hold up a mirror so I can see my entire self, not just the good or not so good areas of growth?
18. Do I genuinely like myself as a person?
19. Do I have integrity in that I am the same person on Friday at Happy Hour as I am when I am at a social event with my family or in church on Sunday?
20. Do I have a sense of humor, especially when it comes to myself and some of my quirky behaviors?

Choosing to live an extraordinary life, means you embrace the idea that it starts with you. Whether it is accountability, responsibility, ownership, happiness, success, or relationships, all the things you want in life start

CHAPTER 16

when you look to yourself to change. Nothing externally will ever fill the gaping hole inside of you unless you do the work to become whole, which is always an inside job.

Loving yourself means that you learn to extend yourself outwardly, beyond the old, tired, untrue, societal, or family-of-origin beliefs that no longer serve you. It means you understand who you are and where your value and worth come from.

It is then you can embrace and love others in an extraordinary way.

CHAPTER 17
EXTRAORDINARY LOVE – OTHERS

I recently was involved in a situation where a friend of mine went back on her word and reneged on an agreement during an incredibly stressful situation.

It wasn't so much her decision as much as it was the way she handled it. This was the second time they had allowed an unresolved problem within their relationship to impact our friendship. Instead of dealing with their relational issues, which always seemed to be a symptom of their own unresolved internal issues, they again chose to avoid them.

When we avoid dealing with our inner issues, they have a way of rearing their ugly heads in our relationships. It doesn't always happen immediately. It happens eventually.

I love the analogy that when you take your hands off the steering wheel, you don't crash immediately…you crash eventually.

The same principal applies regarding loving others. If you don't work through your internal issues, there will always be some form of collateral damage on those around you. At times, it is immediately. At other times, it takes a period of time to unfold. Eventually, however, it is coming soon to a theater near you!

CHAPTER 17

YOUR PAST PREDICTS YOUR FUTURE

Unfortunately, the way most people learned how to do relationships is based on the relationships and behaviors modeled for them as they grew up and through their life experiences. This simply reiterates my point that you must do the work on yourself and work through your issues before you are ready for a relationship. Otherwise, you end up being forced to work through them with a partner who may not be open or want to deal with your issues.

The fact that you selected each other will mean you have issues that are interwoven. We seem to pick partners who present us with our unresolved issues so we can learn to resolve them. When you think about it, you are given the perfect opportunity to work through those issues with them if both parties are conscious, aware, and willing to see it that way.

LOVING YOURSELF IS THE GATEWAY TO LOVING OTHERS

As we mentioned earlier, you can't give away something you don't have, which means you can't fully love someone else until you love yourself. Until we grasp this concept at a heart-felt level, we will continue to run around believing that if we could just find the right person to love, we will finally receive the love we have always desired in return.

I really don't think this is the way it works. In fact, what many people believe is love is what M. Scott Peck would call "cathexis," which is defined as the concentration of mental energy on one particular person, idea, or object (especially to an unhealthy degree). I will add that the concentration on another comes with an expectation of getting something in return. It is a quid pro quo. An example would be, I will treat you nicely if you allow me to control you, so I don't feel insecure about myself. The problem is that no matter how much control a person exerts, it never fills the insatiable hole inside they are trying to fill with another person.

To see this in action, take a long hard look at the love relationships with your friends or family.

Truly loving relationships that are healthy are rare.

EXCESS BAGGAGE CHARGES

We all have known couples who treat each other poorly in public. We see the spouses who try to control their partners out of jealousy—spouses who will attempt to make their partners dependent on them financially or in other ways, so they never leave. Right now, you could probably name one or more couples like this who are really struggling.

So many of these issues could be avoided if folks came into the relationship after at least doing some work on themselves, instead of thinking their partner was the answer to all their problems. When couples move in together, it seems like most just take their baggage from previous relationships (closets) and bring it to the new place (relationship), expecting it to be better or different.

Wouldn't it be better to get rid of the excess baggage *before* you go on your trip instead of dragging it around everywhere you go? Remember you pay extra for overweight baggage and some airlines even you charge you for your carry-on!

Until you have learned how to love yourself, to be in a relationship with yourself, and how to work on becoming the best version of yourself, you will struggle with loving others.

EXTRAORDINARY RELATIONSHIPS

Healthy relationships can happen in two ways. The first option is that you've done your own personal development work, so you begin with the makings for a healthy relationship before you make it permanent. Option two is you both realize you have some relational challenges and realize that you can be mirrors for each other and leverage that concept so that you can develop individually and together.

Option two requires that you make a conscious decision to work on it together, without placing pressure on each other that this must end in reconciliation or a promise to stay together. You must do it to be a better version of yourself first, and a better partner second, which means you have to be willing to sweep your side of the street and tend to your storefront.

The interesting thing about option two is that at times, you will feel and believe you need to point out all your partner's flaws because you don't think your partner has or ever will see them. This, of course, is in lieu of looking at your own flaws with any great depth! Why? Because it feels better and is much easier to focus on the faults of others than it is to own our own faults. This is just human nature.

The problem is that it keeps you in an endless circle of ups and downs, often referred to as "the dance."

SAME OLD SONG AND DANCE

All couples seem to have their own unique dance they keep replaying. The problem is they never learn any new moves, so they stay stuck doing the waltz, the foxtrot, or hip-hop over and over again. It gets old and tiresome, and eventually, they slip into hopelessness and must choose between three options:

1. Continue on this path until it becomes unbearable (see Chapter 7– The 3 Ps of Change – The Pain).
2. Give up and walk away only to continue the same dance with yet another partner—the one that is the complete opposite for the first six months, then magically morphs into the exact same version of every partner you have ever selected, but only this time it is the same issue squared, cubed, or exponentially worse.
3. Seek help from an instructor who can show them how to dance

differently. One of the best resources for beginning this process is the book entitled, *Hold Me Tight,* by Dr. Sue Johnson. It is an invaluable tool to help folks understand the underlying dynamics of the dance as well as how to navigate through it. It is probably one of the best books on the dance I have ever read.

BEYOND YOUR COMFORT ZONES – THE WAY OUT!

If you are willing to take a long, hard look at yourself and work on your issues, the probability that your relationship can work will go up exponentially. This means you will have to be uncomfortable because you will need to examine yourself to understand what you are doing that contributes to the relationship not working.

Where it gets really hard is that you have to be open and willing to own your issues, regardless of whether or not your partner is willing to do the same. It gets very uncomfortable because you must extend yourself, to stretch, and to let go of one trapeze and hang in the air, untethered, alone without a safety net, before you move to the next trapeze.

This is part of becoming a whole person, extending yourself for the sake of your own spiritual growth, and possibly the spiritual growth of another. Remember, as with all things, there are no guarantees.

BEING WILLING AND ABLE

This is why being willing to do what is right for you might mean going it alone, and you may have to go there to save your relationship or your marriage. You may need to have the willingness to let go when you prefer to cling, to own your own stuff regardless of whether anyone else does, and to stretch, push, and go beyond what feels safe, knowing you may end up alone anyway.

If you are willing to allow yourself to be used as a mirror for your partner to see themselves more clearly, without the guarantee that the relationship

CHAPTER 17

will work out, you will discover what it truly means to love one another. The worst thing that can happen is that you lose the relationship, but you learn how to truly love yourself. The best thing that can happen is that you learn from each other how to be the best version of yourselves and therefore partners who understand the true meaning of love—the willingness to extend oneself for the purpose of nurturing the spiritual growth of oneself and another's.

CHAPTER 18
EXTRAORDINARY WORK

When work is a pleasure, life is joy! When work is a duty, life is slavery.

Maxim Gorky

L-O-V-E WHAT YOU DO

We have all read the many surveys from BlessingWhite and Gallup that seem to have been brought up in every single employee engagement blog or conversation. The Covid-19 pandemic has magnified this issue with what has become *The Great Resignation,* as people have simply quit their jobs and no longer want to work or are seeking work somewhere else.

Folks have been disengaged at work for years, and it is costing billions of dollars off the bottom-lines of organizations everywhere! This issue has only magnified over the last few years and is being felt all over the world as employers struggle to attract and retain employees.

If employee engagement and job satisfaction are directly linked to profitability, you would think that most leaders in an organization would have a plan in place to improve it and they would be held accountable for implementing that plan. However, a survey of leaders showed that 75 percent of them had no engagement plan or strategy, even though 90 percent said engagement impacts business success. (ACCOR) This brings me to the ever-important, critical core of the issue—a question we should all be asking ourselves:

Who is ultimately responsible for your level of engagement and satisfaction at work?

The truth is that if you don't like your job, it is *not* the responsibility of your boss, your company, your co-workers, your peers, or anyone else to make you happy. That is on you!

We have become a society where we believe our happiness is the responsibility of everyone but ourselves. The institutions that want to be in control promote the belief that you need them to take care of you. This belief is the root cause of most people's unhappiness and why they outwardly project their unhappiness on statues we need to tear down, violent protests, the media, the government, religious institutions, Pepe Le Pew, and pretty soon, the Muppets and other things like it.

It is a complete and total relinquishment of our responsibility to ourselves and our fellow human beings to evolve, develop, and grow. We scream about our rights and freedom, then we hand the remote control for our brains and our emotions to the government, the media, and religious institutions.

If you choose an external blaming mindset, relying on others to make you happy, I can guarantee that you will be 100 percent miserable for the rest of your life. When it comes to your work, if you do not love what you do or you are dissatisfied with your work, you pretty much have three options:

1. You could quit, walk away, throw in the towel, surrender, give in, and find a position that is better suited for you, your values, and your needs. Just remember if you are currently blaming everyone else for your unhappiness, you will probably bring this to the next position. It is just a matter of time before you are unhappy again.

2. You could stay where you are and keep focusing on what you don't like, what's wrong, and what other folks should be doing so you can be happier at work. Of course, this will just perpetuate your unhappy condition.
3. You could first look at yourself and what you might be contributing to your unhappiness. This requires a shift in your perspective and is always the first step to take before you decide to leave. It requires that you take a long, hard look at what you believe about yourself and your work.

If you conclude that you are 100 percent responsible for your happiness at work, taking a long, hard honest look at yourself without blaming yourself or anyone else while looking for a solution, you are in a much better place to make a business decision from the three options above. This is better than making an emotional decision where your emotions overrule your logic and sound business judgment.

If you are looking for a solution, just remember my mentor Dr. Nido Qubein's words when he said:

> *"Problem solving is looking at what it is, solution finding is looking at what it could be."*

Once you own what your work is, you can look at who you are working with, including yourself!

LOVING WHO YOU DO IT WITH – INSIDE AND OUT

You cannot despise who you are internally and be happy in your work. You have to be content with yourself. Sometimes it is easy to displace the dissatisfaction we have with ourselves and project it on things like our jobs, our bosses, and our co-workers.

So many people are unhappy or discontent with themselves, but they are unwilling to acknowledge it. It is much easier to project our inner angst on others and blame them. In some crazy way, it masks the true issue and tricks us into believing everyone else is the cause of our discontentment.

It is critically important that we are content with ourselves if we are to be content with others. If we don't like ourselves, we won't like our work, and we more than likely won't like the people we work with or for.

I have found that contentment with yourself is directly correlated to the level of clarity you have about your purpose and what you want in life. This is why we spent Chapters 8 through 11 emphasizing the importance of knowing what you want, your purpose, and how to change to achieve the results you desire.

If you are still unclear on your purpose or how to change, this might be a great time to go back and review those chapters. If you reread Chapters 8 through 11, you will do it with a greater awareness and a new set of eyes because you learned even more about yourself from your takeaways in what you have read so far.

Looking at what you need to change to love yourself and your work is the second step in being happy at work.

LOVING WHERE YOU DO IT

At the time this book was being written, we were knee-deep in trying to navigate through the Covid-19 pandemic swamp. Not only did Covid wreak havoc on our lives personally, but it also seriously changed the way we approached work.

Millions of folks who never had the opportunity to work from home were suddenly forced home. The fact that we had no choice has forever changed our societal belief about working from home versus reporting to an office building and being observed under the watchful eye of management.

Unfortunately for some, they were home with their partners, spouses, and children. While this was a great experience for some folks, it was extremely difficult for others.

I don't want to generalize, but in talking with my clients, there seemed to be a split into two camps. On one extreme, the introverts loved the experience. At the other end of the spectrum, the extroverts, who missed the interaction with others, loathed it. For others, it was extremely difficult to separate work life from home life without a boundary or distance to separate them.

To add insult to injury and make matters even worse, we didn't change or alter our approach when it came to our interactions (conducting meetings). We simply conducted three- and four- hour meetings over Zoom or Microsoft Teams as if we were all sitting in a conference room.

Again, the key is to understand and be rock-solid in knowing who you are (purpose) and what you love to do (brilliance and genius). If you can get clarity on these points first, it will result in three outcomes:

1. You will increase the potential to love what you do more readily.
2. You will be more selective in choosing the work you do before leaping or changing positions.
3. You will be more tolerant of the other aspects of your work (with who and where) if you love what you do.

Sometimes we are completely misaligned with who we are and what we do. Sometimes it is a matter of shifting our mindset so we can see our work from a different perspective. Remember our brains are wired to focus on the negative and what is wrong instead of on what is working or is right. Below are five ideas you can implement to increase your level of happiness at work:

1. Sit down and physically write out what really works about your job. This may include all the things your job provides so you can support yourself and your family.
2. List all the reasons that make you a great fit for this job.

3. Answer this question: If I were giving 110 percent effort at work, what would I be doing, doing different, or continuing to do, then immediately start implementing those changes into your daily activities.

4. Set a target productivity level, a sales goal, a promotion, completion of a project, and then focus all of your energy on achieving that target.

5. Set a realistic time frame to accomplish this target. And when you achieve it, one of three things will happen:

    a. You will be rewarded for your achievements.

    b. You will be happier because you were more focused and more productive.

    c. You will be crystal clear that you need find a new position or organization that better aligns with who you are and what you want to be doing in this area of your life. The bonus: your recent achievements will look great on your resume.

When it is all said and done, nobody is responsible for your happiness at work—even though, most of the time, people fail to look at themselves and what they may or may not be doing that is contributing to the problems or misalignments.

Spinning in circles by rehashing all the misgivings and wrongdoings of yourself and/or others, instead of moving toward a solution, will never move you to a point of contentment or happiness at work or in life.

Loving your work is up to you. I have learned that wherever you go, there you are, which happens to be the title of a book by Jon Kabat-Zinn, PhD.[8] Basically, if you have issues and problems and simply switch companies, your issues and problems will be right there with you. I have learned that many times, those issues and problems are magnified in the next location because it is a lesson you need to learn. Resolving your issues and working on yourself is part of your work—your life's work.

Still need more help?

Think back to the chapters on change, where pain is an opportunity to wake you up and move you closer to your purpose. In other words, this may be a great time to look at the problems or challenges you are currently facing and ask yourself, "What do I need to learn about myself from this situation? Where is my vision blurry or out-of-focus?" You might be amazed at how this shift in perception could change your level of happiness, especially at work!

CHAPTER 19
EXTRAORDINARY INSIGHT

GO TO THE MIRROR, BOY!

I might be dating myself here, and yet I think this analogy is strikingly accurate. Back in the late 1960s the British rock band, The Who, released their fourth album entitled, *Tommy*. It was billed as a rock opera and tells the story of a boy whose mother convinces him that he did not see his father (returning from war) killed in an altercation with her lover. Young Tommy sees this, but his mother convinces him that he is deaf, dumb, and blind. The mother spends most of the movie taking Tommy to various quacks and characters who promise to return him back to normal.

At one point they take him to a doctor who says all his tests were normal. "His eyes can see, his ears can hear, and his lips can speak." The doctor goes on to say that he can do nothing and that "all hope…lies within him!" There is one point where the doctor shouts (sings), "Go to the mirror, boy!" The doctor stands him in front of a mirror so he can see himself and a breakthrough ensues. He now sees, feels, and unlocks the key to his awakening. How? By seeing his reflection in the mirror! He is awakened!

So what does this have to do with extraordinary insight? Everything!

For us to truly grow, we need to have the ability to see ourselves as we truly are. However, while most folks love to see their positive traits, most folks do not like seeing the not-so-positive ones. So what do we do? We simply create a way to get rid of them!

Projection is a defense mechanism where we take a part of us that we don't like (i.e., our arrogant-self, selfish-self, or our untrusting-self, etc.) and project it onto someone else.

For example, if we look at someone and say, "What a self-centered person," while there may be a hint of truth in that statement, the full truth is that we, at times, are self-centered as well. The fact is that we don't like it, so we try to rid ourselves of the feeling by projecting our self-centeredness as far away from ourselves as possible.

That concept might be shocking to you. But being conscious of this fact can be incredibly insightful to the areas where we need to develop ourselves. If we fail to pay attention to the feedback of what we project onto others, we miss an opportunity to gain extraordinary insight into ourselves.

If you want to live a truly extraordinary life you must be willing to embrace all of you, not just the great parts. How else can we move beyond the self-inflicted obstacles we place in our very own paths? The willingness to see all of us, our greatness as well as our not-so-greatness, is just another key to unlock the door to our extraordinary life.

The challenge is that this shift requires a significant change in how you navigate through this world. It requires the humility to see ourselves as we really are and to be open to embracing all of us. This is not something easily done, especially if your sense of self-worth and value is derived externally. Whether based on the approval of others, how much money they make, or the toys or the house that possesses them, being externally wired for self-worth and value creates an identity that is quite fragile. This limits a persons' ability to embrace all parts of themselves, especially the negative traits.

Much has been written about owning our not-so-great parts that are often referred to as our shadow. For a more in-depth look at this concept, I suggest a book by Robert A. Johnson, entitled, *Owning Your Own Shadow*.

SEEING MORE OF YOU SO I CAN SEE MORE OF ME

While all this talk about projection can be construed as a complete downer, there is good news about projection.

Projection is a two-way mirror, meaning that if we trust the idea that people are mirrors for us, they can also reflect to us our great traits too! Projection gives us insight into our whole self—all the good and the not so good!

Here's how it works. Write down answers to the following:

1. Name a person you truly admire.
2. What is it about this person you admire most?
3. List at least five characteristics or traits you love about this person.

The interesting fact about this exercise is that those characteristics are just a reflection of the characteristics within you! In fact, the things you wrote down are more about you then they are about the other person.

The question is: Do you believe it? If so, are you truly bringing those characteristics to light and embracing them. Or do you sweep them under the carpet for fear of being arrogant or self-centered?

Yes, what we project on others may just be a mere image of ourselves that we ignore, or it just might be a mirror image revealing one more aspect of your path to living an extraordinary life!

Either way, it is something worth reflecting on.

CHAPTER 20
EMBRACING EXTRAORDINARY RISK

When it comes to discussing Extraordinary Risk, I think it is important to understand how we define risk.

Risk - \'risk\: noun. A situation involving exposure to danger. Verb. Exposing someone or something to danger, harm, or loss.

Risk seems to be associated with danger, hazard, menace, peril, pitfall, threat, or trouble. Interestingly, a mentor of mine once told me that business was about managing risk. It was about deciding where and when to invest your time, energy, or resources to get the greatest return-on-investment. Risk big, win big; risk little, win little. He never talked about avoiding it. He talked about how to manage it!

So why do some folks avoid risk more than others?

THREE FACTORS THAT DETERMINE YOUR PROPENSITY TO RISK

A. Your Personality Style: At one end of the spectrum there is the Type-A, Driver personality who embraces risk. These personality types seek the edge, and they consistently push beyond it. They embrace risk. In fact, they thrive on it. But they can run into problems when they act before they think through a process fully and end up stumbling over unseen or unplanned obstacles, which can challenge them even more to work harder and persist longer to win, overcome adversity, or beat the odds.

The other end of the spectrum is the analytical thinker. For the most part they are risk-adverse. They don't embrace it, they attempt to outthink it. They analyze, over-analyze, and put off decisions until they can collect enough data to ensure that their decisions are risk-free. They paralyze themselves in the indecision mode. They might fail putting themselves or their resources out there, even though a measured incremental bit of risk would provide a new level of success or return.

At any given time, each of us lie somewhere between one end of the spectrum and the other. The actions we take depend on our personality type, the perceived risk, or our past experiences.

B. Your Past Experience: In life, we all have experiences that we wish we could forget. We believe that if we could have avoided that incident, our lives may have turned out much better. At times, we fail to realize that the unfortunate experience could be one of our greatest life lessons, which begs the questions:

Why is it that some folks seem to be able to pick themselves up, move on, and try again? They learn a valuable lesson from the miscue and then leverage the learning to propel themselves forward.

Why is it that some folks come to a stop and never move forward or try again? They stay stuck, living in the past and fearing that they may repeat the same bad experience.

The unfortunate thing about the second group is that they end up living in the past. They are ladened with regret, which slowly robs them of the new opportunities to live an extraordinary life! You hear them say things like, "I tried that once, I'll never try that again. I've always done it this way, I am who I am, my dad was an alcoholic, my mother was distant and cold, etc."

The path out is to understand and embrace the idea that life deals us some good and not so good situations or circumstances. You want to embrace both and realize that one cannot exist without the other. It would be like trying to experience day without night. It is impossible, so why fight it?

C. Your Personal Belief Systems: As we discussed in Chapter 9, the belief exists that while we are in our mothers' womb we are being influenced by our mothers' beliefs. If you have a mother who is fear-based, risk-adverse, or just an overall worrier, her body releases chemicals like epinephrine, cortisol, and adrenaline, which enters the fetus. Now imagine a baby who gets a steadfast diet of these chemicals because of the mother being fear-based? The long-term effects can be disastrous on the child with far reaching implications well into adulthood.

Remember, once we are born, we get imprinted very early with our parent's beliefs about God, relationship, family, money, culture, sex, etc. Eventually we attend school, and again, we get imprinted by those in authority: our teachers, pastors, priests, rabbi, imam, etc. If you consider our personality styles and life experiences (including education), you have the formation of your personal belief system.

Our personal belief system plays a critical role in how we navigate life. One of the single biggest factors which determines our course in life is our willingness to risk. Choosing to live an extraordinary life means that we move beyond what is known, common, safe, and comfortable. It means we must risk and consistently go outside of what is ordinary, common, and comfortable. Whether it is a giant leap or a baby step, as long as you consistently move forward you will achieve your version of living an extraordinary life.

OBSTACLES – YOUR OLD NEMESIS

If you find yourself stuck, unwilling to step beyond your comfort zone, more than likely you will find your old nemesis lurking somewhere in the shadows. Your fear!

Remember, Swiss Psychiatrist, Carl Jung, once said, "It is not what it is, it is what we make it mean!" It is how we define fear, risk, and comfort.

Napoleon Hill is a famous American self-help author whose book, *Think and Grow Rich* (1937) is among the ten best-selling self-help books of all time. He said, "Fears are nothing more than a state of mind!"

Basically, both of these brilliant people are saying the same thing. Fear is what you make it mean! Now imagine how empowered you would be if you embraced this simple idea that you choose how you navigate through fear.

You can overcome your fear and lead the way to living an extraordinary life or you can let it paralyze you into living a fear-based, ordinary, common life. It is a choice—it is *your* choice—even if it at times it can appear overwhelming. The reality of today's culture is that fear is peddled non-stop, 24/7, on every news channel and media outlet. You have to be even more diligent to pry yourself away from the prison cell that living in fear creates.

If you were to look at your level of happiness in some of the key areas of your life and rate them, how would you score?

In fact, take out a sheet of paper and on the left column vertically, write down the following categories: Finances, Career, Personal Growth, Family, Friends, Relationships, Spiritual, Fun/Recreation, and Health and Wellness. Now score each category by writing a number between 1 and 10, with 1 being low and 10 being high on your level of happiness in each category. In the next column, rank your willingness to take risk on a similar scale from 1 to 10 in each of these areas.

I'm sure you will see a correlation to the level of happiness and the level of risk you are willing to take. And while that is important, what is even more important is asking yourself what you want to do about it.

If you were to select just one area, the area that you feel would have the single biggest positive impact on your life, which would you choose?

Then decide what small step you could take to move that area of your life to the next level.

What is interesting about this exercise is that you already knew this, but you were just not in a place to take action.

CHAPTER 21
EXTRAORDINARY WISDOM

Honesty is the first chapter in the book of wisdom.

Thomas Jefferson

Throughout history, much has been written on the topic of wisdom. It has been studied, analyzed, and dissected for thousands of years. Attempts to put it in motion have been unfolding for hundreds of years before the birth of Christ and continue for thousands of years after his death. We even created an entire academic discipline devoted to the study of wisdom. We call it philosophy.

Still today, we argue back and forth over major and minor ideas, thoughts, philosophical positions, differences, and beliefs. All this is in an effort to appear wise or at least more wise than someone else, usually another person with an opposing idea from an opposing tribe or party.

History shows us wars that were waged because of the ill-fated wisdom of dictators who at first appeared to be wise, so people followed them—often blindly—only to discover that, in the end, they were anything but wise. They were just experts at stirring up emotions of separation, exclusion, and hatred.

It is safe to say that over the course of the last twelve months of 2020 and the first few months of 2021, as the world was stricken by a pandemic, we were disappointed at the lack of wisdom from a few of our fellow human beings, whether it was watching riots and protests for one cause or another, mass lootings, or the simple act of saying, "You can't make me wear a mask. I am an American, and I have rights!" We completely ignored the fact that their unwise behaviors were stomping on the rights of their fellow human beings.

Today, I believe most of us hope and pray that we find some level of common sense amongst ourselves and the worlds' leaders, especially those leaders in our nation's capital.

WISDOM AND THE HUMAN RACE

I could write an entire book on what's wrong in the world or about the lack of wisdom and common sense. However, for the purposes of this book, I want to share five thoughts about wisdom so we can better understand why wisdom is a fundamental component in our evolution as human beings. We should also understand why it is a critical factor that impacts your ability to live an extraordinary life!

1. The basic definition of wisdom is simply the ability to think and act using knowledge, experience, understanding, common sense, and insight.
2. The word "sapience" is derived from the Latin word *sapientia*, which means wisdom.
3. *Homo* in Latin is the noun for "man," like in "mankind."
4. We define ourselves as *homo sapiens*.
5. We are supposed to be wise—wise men, wise women, and wise people.

In other words, the very basis of how we define who we are as human beings is intricately interwoven and inseparable from the belief that we obtain wisdom and act wisely, but what happens when you turn on the news or log into Facebook or any social media site?

What you see is manipulation by people with agendas and beliefs all claiming they are wise. They couldn't be any further from the truth. They all seem to lack wisdom. Why? Because they are driven by a purpose that is diametrically opposed to the ideas of inclusion, common sense, understanding, knowledge, and insight.

It is important to separate conventional wisdom from what has been defined as alternative wisdom. At some point in history, the conventional wisdom of the day said the earth was flat. Galileo, known as the "father" of observational astronomy, believed the earth was round and that it revolved around the sun. It took courage and chutzpah to go outside the conventional (cultural, institutional) wisdom of the Catholic Church to stand up for what he believed. After he was convicted of heresy, he spent the rest of his life under house arrest, essentially imprisoned.

Conventional wisdom, the beliefs of the herd, or the common beliefs of the culture, are not always filled with wisdom. Sometimes they are simply another form of imprisonment.

WISDOM: YOUR FUNDAMENTAL RESPONSIBILITY

Of course, it is easy to point fingers at those in power and blame them for the chaos and disruption. I believe that most folks would rather give away that responsibility, simply take a chair, and participate in a game of follow the leader. It is easier to blame someone else when things go wrong. Pointing our fingers outward and away from ourselves instead of inward seems to be a basic human foible. It would appear that, as human beings, we have an unconscious need to shun responsibility.

That said, as homo sapiens and members of the human race, it is *our* responsibility to apply wisdom, common sense, and understanding to ourselves and each other. If we stop acquiring wisdom, if we give away our responsibility to act wisely, we are dismissing our right to be human, and we basically sell ourselves out!

It is our individual responsibility as human beings to be wise, act wisely, and continuously seek wisdom that goes beyond what everyone believes. We must be even more diligent in these modern times, ladled with manipulated facts, stories, images from the media, and of course, the ever-invasive reach of social media, which seems to be seeping into every crack and crevice of our daily lives.

In chaotic times, it is even more important that we take responsibility for our beliefs, our behaviors, and therefore the results we are achieving in our lives. It is not only your responsibility. It is also your obligation as a member of the human race.

THE RELATIONSHIP BETWEEN WISDOM, HONESTY, AND EGO

If we are to be wise and act wisely, we must be able to discern and judge what is true and what is right. Thomas Jefferson, in this chapter's opening quote, identifies the causal relationship between honesty and wisdom. You cannot have wisdom without honesty, first and foremost with yourself and then with others.

At first take, getting honest with ourselves seems simple. While seemingly the concept is simple, it is not easy. Scientific research tells us that we all believe we are much more honest than we are.

It is hard because honesty requires a willingness to seek the truth in any and every situation, regardless of your predetermined beliefs or conditioning. This means you must go beyond the barriers your ego creates to protect your inner sense so as to maintain what you project outwardly to others. The biggest factor preventing us from seeing ourselves honestly is that we don't like change, especially when it comes to changing ourselves.

Although we dislike change, our ego despises it. Our ego is more invested in keeping things just the way they are, and it attributes change with being wrong, flawed, bad, or less than perfect.

Obtaining wisdom requires a deep level of honesty. When honesty goes up, wisdom goes up. When honesty takes a nose-dive, so does our ability to think and act wisely. Increasing our wisdom requires taking a long hard look into the areas of our lives where we are missing the mark. Once we identify those areas, we simply need to admit that we are misaligned with who or what we want to be. It is important to make sure we do not make ourselves bad or wrong, nor that we shovel heaps of shame and guilt upon ourselves. We simply need to admit we are misaligned.

In Chapter 4, I stated that the biggest obstacle to change was our ego. I also shared in Chapter 5, that to move forward, we needed to dissolve our egos. This is done by letting go of our desire to be in control and be right. The remedy was large doses of humility and acceptance.

If we can reduce our dependency on the ego, we can begin to be honest with ourselves and each other. This is the path to wisdom. You can't get there if you allow your ego to keep tripping you up.

There is an inverse correlation between the ego and wisdom. When ego goes up, wisdom goes down. When wisdom goes up, the ego is diminished. If your ego is overinflated due to a need to protect your beliefs and your sense of self-worth and value, you will be blinded from the truth about yourself and others.

It becomes a matter of seeking the truth! So where do we go to discover our truth?

CHAPTER 22
EXTRAORDINARY HONESTY

SEEKING THE WHOLE TRUTH AND NOTHING BUT THE TRUTH

Deciding what *the truth* is gets a bit tricky for me. How do I discern what is true? How do I know what is right, according to who?

What we were taught, how and where we were raised, and our level of education and experiences form how we see the world and what we determine is real. That becomes our version of reality, our version of what is true and right. This means we all hold differing beliefs and we all have different versions of the truth. A young girl raised in Uganda and a young boy raised in the Upper East Side of New York City will have vastly different versions of reality and, therefore, what they believe to be the truth.

So where or to whom do you turn to find the truth—the media, your parents, your politicians, your peers, your church, Alexa? Does this mean you decide what is right or true?

We all know people who can justify behaviors we find to be quite far from the "truth" or what we believe to be "right." Haven't we all, at one time or another, justified behaviors in our past that we now know were not healthy or harmed others? Haven't we all made wrong choices at times?

Even if we have acquired some amount of wisdom, it doesn't guarantee that we will always act wisely. We all know very wise people, who at different times, made some very unwise decisions.

THE DUALISTIC MINDSET

History shows us that disparities in defining what is the truth is at the core of most, if not all, conflicts. Much of what folks argue about is defending their beliefs about what is true or right. While some issues can be resolved with this either-or mindset, the more complex issues cannot.

We refer to this either-or type of thinking as a dualistic mindset. Dualistic thinking assumes a world where there are only two possible mutually-exclusive choices. It means that we see some*thing* or some*one* as either all good or all bad, all right or all wrong, all good or all evil, and all positive or all negative. Complex issues and challenges cannot be solved with black-and-white, cut and dried, and either-or thinking. Life in all its complexity really isn't that simple, even though we would like it to be.

The decision whether to walk in front of a speeding vehicle at a crosswalk should be a simple clear-cut decision. The decision whether we should drink cyanide should be as clear-cut as whether we walk in front of a speeding car. In both situations, the answer should be a resounding *hell no*, but history has taught us that when you add complex factors or issues into the mix—religion, politics, human nature, relationships, and especially God—bad decisions can be made, unwise outcomes can happen, and sometimes horrific tragedies can take place.

DUALITY AND COMPLEX ISSUES

On November 18, 1978, in Jonestown, Guyana, 909 people including 304 children died of an apparent mass suicide by ingesting cyanide. The founder, Jim Jones, died of an apparent self-inflicted gunshot wound. This all unfolded just hours after U.S. Representative Leo Ryan was killed on the airstrip in Guyana while attempting to leave. He was there to investigate claims that U.S. citizens were being held against their will.

What might be a simple yes-or-no decision for you and me became a convolution of religious and political beliefs resulting in a horrific tragedy. The point here is not to discuss the morality of Jonestown, even though the conclusion drawn seems obvious. The point here is how our own individual or group beliefs can drive us to make incredibly unwise decisions.

When we are emphatic about our beliefs, when we believe them to be the absolute truth, we limit our ability to see the bigger picture.

To say any group, race, political party, country, etc. that doesn't align with our beliefs are evil and we are all good is simply not the truth. All we are doing is projecting our beliefs on the world so we can feel better about ourselves and above our fellow humans. While it may feel good in the short-term, we drastically reduce our ability to possess the wisdom needed to find a mutually-inclusive solution to the problem or issue.

We human beings take great pride in placing labels on people and things and placing them in finite boxes. For some reason, it makes us feel safe, right, better than, etc. It does nothing to move us forward as *homo sapiens*, as wise people, or as members of this human race.

Question to Reflect: Where in my life am I applying an either-or, black-or-white, exclusionary mindset to a more complex issue?

In what areas or situations of my life do I need to think in a different and more extraordinary way?

These questions will help you discern where you go to establish the truth or what is right for you. The idea is to discern whether you are willing to examine how you seek the truth and what is right. This plays an import role in how you evolve your beliefs and the system of beliefs that drives your actions.

CHAPTER 22

THREE QUESTIONS TO ASK YOURSELF ABOUT TRUTH AND HONESTY:

1. How do you discern what is real and what is not when it comes to discerning the truth?
2. How much of what you believe is simply a regurgitation of what you see on the television or read on social media?
3. Do you decide the truth based on your experience or on what someone else tells you?

CHAPTER 23
EXTRAORDINARY THINKING

We cannot solve our problems with the same thinking we used when we created them.

Albert Einstein

A MOST EXTRAORDINARY THINKER

One of the people I admire most is Albert Einstein. Over the course of many years, I have quoted him quite often. This is partially because of his ability to think in an incredibly balanced way. He always seemed to encompass both the analytical-left and creative-right hemispheres of the brain in an uncanny and extraordinary way.

After his death at the age of 76, his brain was removed and studied. What they discovered was an enlarged area of the brain connecting the left and right hemispheres. It is referred to as the "corpus callosum." When this part of the brain functions well, the brain can generate, retrieve, retain, and transform well-structured visual images. An enlarged corpus callosum also indicate an extremely high level of both verbal and social levels of reasoning (emotional intelligence).

He has been referred to as the master of both dualistic and non-dualistic thinking. His ability to understand, perceive, act, and know when to apply non-dualistic and dualistic thinking was nothing less than extraordinary.

In order to create, imagine, and go beyond the limits of his thinking, he had constantly to push beyond what he knew to be true based on what he saw with his eyes. He opened his mind to see beyond what was and into the possibility of what could be, even though it was unthinkable or unimaginable to others, especially his peers.

In his quest to push the limits of his thinking and ours, he became one of the most prominent thinkers of all time.

What does this mean for you and I and our thinking? As I have mentioned previously, it is your beliefs that drive your behaviors and are wielding the results you are achieving in your life.

Your collective beliefs are the foundation of your internal belief system. They are all viewed through the lenses of your perception and dramatically influence how you make your way in the world. Most of us formulate our belief systems over time, but at some point, we stop formulating or reformulating, and they become stagnant. We get comfortable in knowing what we know or believing what we believe. We walk through the world with our belief systems painted on a canvas we carry alongside us. As we walk, we compare what we see in the world to our internal beliefs and then judge the person, place, or thing as good or bad, right or wrong, etc. Basically, it's dualistic thinking!

When we get stuck, hit a roadblock, or are not achieving what we want, we apply our current level of thinking even harder or shut out other ideas and beliefs even more. We then wonder why nothing changes and we continue to achieve the same less-than-desired results. In other words, we apply the same thinking (beliefs) to the situation that created the problem in the first place. Then we don't understand why nothing changes.

We fail to open ourselves up to thinking beyond what we currently believe, think, know, or imagine. We wait until the pain of change cracks us open before we open ourselves to the possibility that there might be another way, approach, or mindset. Unfortunately, this is why in order for most people to change, they must experience pain.

If you want to live an extraordinary life, you have to be willing go outside of your current thinking and beliefs to see the bigger picture.

Let's look at this a different way.

BLACK, WHITE, AND GRAY

Let's say I stand you in a room made up of four identically-sized walls, each one measuring 10 by 25 feet or 250 sq. ft. per wall. Now let's say I hand you a gallon of white paint (one gallon covers 250 sq. ft.) and ask you to paint one wall. How much of that one wall could you cover all in white? The answer is 250 sq. ft. Now I hand you a gallon of black paint and ask you to repeat the exercise on another wall. How much of that second wall could you cover all in black? Yes, another 250 sq. ft. Now let's say I hand you one gallon of black paint and one gallon of white paint and ask you to paint the remaining two walls one color. What would you do? You would have to mix the black and white paints together to make gray and then you could cover the remaining 500 square feet!

Get the point?

The picture you see, the area you can cover, expands immensely when you can see beyond black and white, beyond all good and all evil, and all right and all wrong, when you encompass a wider view or perspective.

Being an extraordinary thinker means that we must transform our thinking, examine our beliefs, and open ourselves up to the possibility that there is some truth beyond what we currently believe or think. It means we have to let go—stop wasting time labeling things and people and putting them in boxes—so we can keep them outside and away from us just to feel safe. It means we stop excluding others and look for ways that include them. It means we stop living in a constant state of fear, excommunicating or condemning anyone who doesn't believe what we believe. We stop creating imaginary enemies and find a way that benefits all of us, not just me and my tribe.

Imagine if you could step back from your dualistic, black-or-white, good or bad, right or wrong thinking, and see the grayness of the issues you face. Imagine an inner world where you have the ability to think and see beyond your challenges to a bigger, broader, more expansive way of thinking? Now imagine if everyone solved their problems in this manner of extraordinary thinking.

Imagine if this shift away from dualistic thinking to a non-dualistic mindset was prevalent in Washington D.C., the United Nations, or the local church? Imagine if this non-dualistic thinking was the overall mindset on social media, the media, classrooms, the pulpit, the synagogue, the temple, or the mosque? Wouldn't that be extraordinary?

This is what it means to be an extraordinary thinker—*homo sapiens* and a wise person.

Being an extraordinary thinker begins when you take a deep long hard look inside.

THE SCIENCE BEHIND BLINDING YOURSELF

If we take a deep, long, hard look at ourselves, we need to be sure that we are seeing ourselves clearly. By that, I mean we must see ourselves without our lenses of perception being clouded or smudged, even when our physiology influences us in a way that alters the way we see things.

Scientists have discovered that we are attracted to negative thoughts much easier than positive thoughts. It is referred to as a "negative response bias," and our brains are wired in this manner. Some scientists believe that it is an age-old mindset because for millions of years, we have been forced to guard against life-threatening instances or situations.

Our brain actually releases negative chemicals (cortisol) much more freely than the positive chemicals (dopamine) as a way to protect us. The sense of anxiety we experience when we feel a threat while driving is actually hard-wired into our brains. The amygdala or the reptilian part of our brain which regulates emotion (fight or flight) uses approximately 66 percent of its neurons focusing on negative events or emotion. It is a response that will actually increase the cortisol levels in our brains. The same can be said about the buzz (dopamine) we feel when our text alarm goes off and we get excited to read it.

Now the science behind this isn't as important as what you do to prevent all the good egg stuff from spilling out of your brain while it clings to the scary, always on-guard, fear-based thoughts that plague us throughout our day. This will definitely impact the way you see yourself and the way you see others.

Being intentional in reprogramming your brain to focus on what is good—especially when surrounded by the media, which always seems to focus on the bad—requires being focused and intentional. It is also incredibly healthy.

You can never completely wipeout all negative thoughts or feelings, and why would you? Negative thoughts are not bad unless you wallow in them. They can help us determine whether we go left or right, up or down, or determine which action to take.

Being aware enough to know if your brain is biased toward the negative is important in determining whether you're seeing things clearly. Negativity bias, driven by fear, can blind you from seeing the bigger picture or taking risks, and therefore prevent you from living an extraordinary life.

Positive thoughts don't exist without negative thoughts, just as the color black doesn't exist without white. Seeing beyond the black and white creates a broader spectrum of possibilities.

CHAPTER 23

A PLACE TO START

To begin, you have to answer the following questions honestly:

1. Are you willing to let go of your need to be right, be liked, win, or be seen a certain way?
2. Are you open and willing to possibly let go of what you were taught when it comes to the absolute no-holes barred truth?
3. Are you willing to own that the change needing to happen is in you first and foremost and not the rest of the world?

If you cannot honestly answer yes to all three questions, I suggest you put the book down and go find a quiet place to sit and reflect on this thought:

> Am I willing to see the truth about me—the true me, the real me, the me I am when no one else is around and I am alone with my thoughts, fears, addictions, and self-doubt, without the facades and masks I present to the world?

I can already sense your ego clamping down, pulling up the drawbridge and wielding the sword and shield, screaming "I go down, you go with me!" Or it might just be a gentle whisper in your ear to forget it, ignore it, run away and pretend you've never heard any of this. All I can ask is that you sit tight and stay with me.

Start where it counts most. Start by being willing to open up to and see clearly the essence of the most important person in the world.

YOU!

Pull out a sheet of paper. Don't answer these questions in your head, but write down your answers if you want the full impact of this exercise.

Ask yourself these questions:

1. Do I believe that my true self is not the same self I present to others in some but not all areas of my life?

2. Without judging or blaming anyone, can I look at my life and see how many of my actions or behaviors were intended to protect this inner sense of self?
3. Can I look back at my life and see how some of the things I was taught as a child, adolescent, young adult, and even now do not serve me well or in a healthy way?
4. Do any of these beliefs help me to understand or make sense of why I acted or still behave in a way that doesn't really serve me?
5. Sometimes to avoid owning our junk, it is easier to project it onto others. Are there any behaviors I abhor in others? What is it specifically about this persons' behavior I despise most? Is it their arrogance, stubbornness, pride, disrespectfulness, etc.?
6. Where in my life or in what situations did I act in a similar manner or exhibit the very same characteristics I am now judging in this other person?
7. What was my underlying motive? Was I acting from a place of love or was it fear? Remember that anger, most of the time, is just a sub-emotion of fear, even though we all hate to admit we are afraid!
8. In the areas where I have identified my behavior as fear-based, what is it that I am most afraid of?
9. In these situations when I was acting out of a place of fear—when I messed up, screwed up, was embarrassed, or felt like a miserable failure, etc.—what did or would I have wanted someone I trusted to do or say to me?
10. Knowing what you know now (that this is more about you than others) What actions do you need to take going forward to stay out of that negative fear-based thinking? What beliefs might you need to alter, shift, or transform to help you move forward?
11. How can you embed this newfound thinking and behavior into every aspect of your life, especially the areas where you are disturbed, upset, are acting holier-than-thou, or are judging a complex issue in a black-or-white mindset?

Extraordinary thinking doesn't just happen because you read a book, watched a video, or decided to change. It requires an ongoing, consistent level of self-reflection. It requires a high level of trust in what Mahatma Gandhi said about change. "Be the change you wish to see in the world!"

As in most things, it begins when you and I—we, us, the wise people, and the *homo sapiens* who inhabit this planet—decide to shift our thinking. It begins when we take 100 percent responsibility for our thinking and make a constant commitment to moving outside our comfort zones, opening ourselves to seek the truth and being honest with ourselves and each other. It is our continuous quest to seek wisdom. Then and only then can we experience this facet of living an extraordinary life.

CHAPTER 24
EXTRAORDINARY FORGIVENESS

Resentment is like drinking poison and waiting for the other person to die.

Saint Augustine

A CULTURE OF RESENTMENT

One of the most famous lines from a movie describes a lifelong pursuit of revenge in what has become a cult classic for children and adults, *The Princess Bride*. Mandy Patinkin plays Inigo Montoya, a feisty Spaniard whose father was slain by a six-fingered man, Count Rugen, when he was just a small boy. Rugen slashes the boy's cheek, wounding him and leaving a permanent scar on his face externally and on his soul internally, a daily reminder of the incident and a powerful propellant to fuel his anger and resentment.

At one point in the movie, Inigo is finally facing Count Rugen in a sword duel. Rugen is getting the best of him and Inigo is on death's door. Just when you think he is done and his lifelong purpose will go unfulfilled, he awakens. He begins to repeat the line he has rehearsed his entire life, "My name is Inigo Montoya. You killed my father. Prepare to die."

Miraculously, the repeating of this now-famous line brings him back to life! And just like that, he slays Count Rugen and fulfills his life's purpose.

Resentment and family feuds were also at the heart of William Shakespeare's epic love story, *Romeo and Juliet*. Resentment and holding grudges have been a part of and what led to their suicides.

It would seem that resentment and revenge are memes intricately woven into our culture. The *Rambo* series, *Gladiator*, *Braveheart*, *Unforgiven*, *Death Wish*, *The Sting*, *Carrie*, and even the *Karate Kid* are movies about revenge and resentment, and we love them!

Resentment need not always end in death. Growing up in a Sicilian family, resentment-based vendettas are practically a part of the culture. On a smaller scale, they would result in family members not speaking for days, weeks, months, and sometimes years.

OH, THE STORIES WE MAKE UP

Of course, there was always some life-or-death reason that caused the resentment. Someone called someone an Italian expletive, someone didn't bring a gift to the baptism, or the gift was not as expensive as the gift they had given their kid. We can create stories in our heads to justify our behavior no matter how ridiculous it seems.

The human mind is incredibly powerful. It can change, alter, and reshape reality to justify anything. We make up stories in our minds to justify our behavior, even when our behavior results in the death of others. History has shown that human beings can justify the death of others if it serves our needs or desire to control or prove we are right, whether it be the Inquisition or the many wars that have taken place over time.

The point is that we can create any story in our brains and make it mean anything we choose. As we rationalize and bend the truth to our stories, we typically move further and further away from the truth.

The problem is while we believe that we are imparting harm on others, we are instead imparting a slow death on ourselves.

KILLING ME SOFTLY

Our willingness to justify our feelings or emotions is all about serving an internal need or desire to prove we are right, we have been wronged, we are victims, that we are good, and our enemy is evil. When referring to the enemy, I'm referring to anyone who doesn't agree with us.

We hold onto resentments and believe that the resentment is harming others. We run and rerun the verdict from our internal courtroom over and over in our heads, slamming down the gavel and pronouncing the other party guilty as charged, even events that have happened decades in our past. However, we fail to realize that this resentment that we cling to is a poison that we drink while believing that our enemy will die. It is we who are experiencing a slow death. As with many things, death doesn't come immediately, as it is an internal death that happens eventually and over time.

Studies have shown that resentment, anger, and the inability to forgive create a far more negative impact on the holder than the person on whom we project our resentments.[9]

We experience:

- A weakened immune system.
- Adverse impact on sleep.
- Increased blood pressure elevations, increasing the risk of heart disease and stroke.
- Increase in our inflammatory response increasing risk for heart disease, cancer, diabetes, arthritis, skin conditions, and more.
- Lower energy levels.
- Higher rates of depression.
- The possibility of digestive or eating problems.

The short burst we get from our ego when we feel right certainly doesn't outweigh the negative impacts on our bodies and minds, but we continue to hold onto these negative feelings and resentments as if our life depended on it, when all along, our life depends on letting them go.

FORGIVENESS – THE PATH TO FREEDOM

While there are many definitions of forgiveness, the two that captures the essence of the point I am trying to make are the following:

1. to give up all claim on account of.
2. to cease to feel resentment against someone or something.

When we can give up our claim to continue repeating the accusation of guilt in our head to prove our rightness and their wrongness, it is not about forgetting; it is about moving beyond your pain. When we forgive, we are refusing to live in the past hurts. We are refusing to continue damaging our mental, physical, emotional, and spiritual health.

When we forgive, we are not saying, "I was not hurt, I was not wronged, or it did not happen." We are saying, "I refuse to keep playing the courtroom scene over in my head pretending I am sentencing the other to a life sentence in prison, when in essence I am sentencing myself."

When we forgive, we are setting ourselves free because we cease to hold on to the resentment that is eating us alive from the inside out.

FORGIVENESS AND LIVING AN EXTRAORDINARY LIFE

You cannot live an extraordinary life from a self-imposed prison cell. Living an extraordinary life means you have to go beyond what you think is safe, secure, and comfortable. It is easy to get trapped in a mindset that brings us a sense of temporary relief from our pain. It is analogous to the short-term relief addicts get from using their drug of choice. Resentment can be a drug, and we can be addicted to resentment because like alcohol or meth, it gives us temporary relief from the pain or hurt we don't want to feel.

As with drugs or alcohol, the short-term relief we feel never takes into consideration the long-term damage that is done from our using.

CHAPTER 25
EXTRAORDINARY FREEDOM - PART I

Note: I feel the need to state that I am not a therapist, addictions counselor, or medical professional. I am simply a fellow traveler who felt the need to share his life experience regarding the behaviors, thinking, and attachments that have at times kept me addicted, imprisoned, and not free.

The biggest obstacle I have had to overcome is my fear that underneath all the facades, embedded beliefs, and material things, there was nothing. Translation = I was nothing. Without my house, cars, business, reputation, books, thinking, clients, money, drive, and desire to succeed, I would be of no substance. I would cease to exist.

Breaking free has been and continues to be an ongoing, never-ending process. Every time I feel I have conquered or overcome some obstacle in my life, another appears, and I feel the need to face it.

I am learning that it is not in the holding on to self, thinking, or things that I find freedom, but in the letting go.

I see this as just one more paradox in this thing we call life.

Free·dom|\ 'frē-dəm\[10]

1. the absence of necessity, coercion, or constraint in choice or action.

2. liberation from slavery or restraint or from the power of another: independence.
3. the quality or state of being exempt or released from something oppressive.

CINDERELLA STORY

The 2005 movie, *Cinderella Man*, starring Russell Crowe has one of the most poignant scenes about freedom I have ever seen.

The movie is based on the true story about James J. Braddock, a onetime, pre-depression fighter who gets written off after losing a few matches because he was boxing with a broken hand. That is when things take a turn for the worse.

The depression hits and Braddock's family is living in a cramped one-room, lower-level apartment, with no heat and nothing to eat. His wife Mae (Renee Zellweger) sends his children away to relatives to be cared for because James is unable to pay the bills. This is the last straw, and this humbled but proud man ends up on public assistance and begging for help. He needs money to turn the electricity back on and bring his family back together.

As a result of a chance turn of events, he gets an opportunity to fight again. He is just a placeholder and is expected to lose. Instead, he wins and starts a Cinderella-story comeback all the way to the heavyweight championship and defeats the current champ, Max Baer.

The scene that I find to be so extraordinary takes place after his momentous rise. He returns to the unemployment office to give back every single penny of the money he received while on assistance. The question I ask myself is why? Was he proud? Was he thinking others needed it more than he did?

I believe that James Braddock was a proud man. He took 100 percent responsibility for his life and for his family. He saw the money as a loan, not an entitlement. He just needed a boost up during a tough time. He had a sense of pride and integrity and didn't expect anything for free.

I imagine that had he not paid back the money, it would have haunted him for years. He didn't feel that anyone owed him anything and didn't want to be beholden to anyone else!

He was free!

AMERICA THE FREE

Here in America, we pride ourselves on being free. For nearly 250 years, freedom has been our battle cry whenever we feel that we are being controlled or restricted. We see the battle lines drawn in the media and social media, at cocktail parties and family get-togethers. It is obvious that we here in America hold our freedom in extremely high regard, so much so that we are willing to die for it or kill others. In some ways and for some people, the refusal to be vaccinated had nothing to do with science and everything to do with freedom to choose. It was a 'values' thing and not a 'science' thing.

The truth is that in many ways, when you compare the level of freedom we have in this country to other countries around the world, there can be no denying the fact that we are free from tyranny, dictators, and censorship. We see communist countries such as Russia, China, and North Korea, along with the many restrictions and control they place on their people, and we say, "Never in America because we are free!"

FAUX FREEDOM

There is a faux freedom that we rarely speak about. It is hidden in the background, shrouded by our systems of beliefs, what we truly value, and our desire to do whatever it is we want, whenever we want to do it (freedom of choice)

We demand freedom of speech, yet we allow hate speech because it is our right, whether it infringes on the rights or the freedoms of others to live free of persecution, oppression, or prejudices.

Is freedom for only a select few?

We indulge deeply and post whatever we want on social media only to find that our every move on the internet is under surveillance, being tracked, and watched in order to prostitute out our personal information to the highest bidder. Isn't freedom deciding what we allow others to do with our personal information without coercion or constraint in choice or action?

The Covid pandemic has resulted in stimulus checks being handed out to people who didn't need the money and loans to companies that do not need to be paid back and did not need them. The battle cry was, "If I don't take it, someone else will. I might as well take it."

There is a saying, "There is no such thing as a free lunch." Yet we call this free money, continually kicking the can of debt down the generational ladder and pushing future generations into the oppression of debt they will never get out from under.

How is this different from sharecropping in the Post-Civil War era? Or for hundreds of years prior to that?

We are a nation driven by a system of consumerism. It is our belief that we need to acquire more, even though we have more money and things collectively than any other country in the world. All the while, total household debt has increased to $14.35 trillion, 13.2 percent higher than the peak debt per household during Q3 of 2008, which was the Housing Bubble Crash.[11]

The truth is that in our pursuit of freedom and our quest to have more, we fail to learn our lessons from the past. We have become prisoners of a system that blinds us to our dependencies, and in doing so, we are not free.

ADDICTIONS WE TALK ABOUT

In 2018, 55.2 percent of the adult population (over 18) drank alcohol daily according to 2018 research. In that same year, 11 million Americans over the age of twenty-six met the criteria for alcohol use disorder.

5.5 million people reported misusing prescription hydrocodone in 2018. Doctors prescribed opioids 51.4 times per 100 people in 2018. Synthetic opioids like fentanyl were part of 70 percent of all drug overdose deaths in 2018. 808,000 people reported past-year heroin use in 2018. Almost 15,000 people died from heroin overdoses in 2018.

In 2018, over 106,000 adults used meth on a daily basis, a 43 percent increase compared to the prior year. The same year, 1.6 million adults over age twenty-six reported having used methamphetamine in the past year. Since 2000, over 700,000 Americans have died from drug overdoses. There were over 60,000 drug overdose deaths in the United States in 2018.[12]

The statistics above obviously point to a serious problem. The Covid-19 pandemic, if anything, increased the use of drugs, alcohol, and other behaviors associated with being addicted.

"According to the Centers for Disease Control and Prevention, as of June 2020, 13 percent of Americans reported starting or increasing substance use as a way of coping with stress or emotions related to COVID-19. Overdoses have also spiked since the onset of the pandemic. A reporting system called ODMAP shows that the early months of the pandemic brought an 18 percent increase nationwide in overdoses compared with those same months in 2019. The trend has continued throughout 2020, according to the American Medical Association, which reported in December that more than 40 U.S. states have seen increases in opioid-related mortality along with ongoing concerns for those with substance use disorders."[13]

ADDICTIONS WE DON'T TALK ABOUT

If we are to grasp this immense concept of addiction, we must go outside of what we traditionally hold and internalize it. We must be willing to look at any substance, behavior, or process that keeps you bound. This is a far broader definition than what we typically label as addictions (typically drugs and alcohol).

Below is a short list of things people can be addicted to. While not exhaustive, it puts into context the point I am attempting to make:

Drugs, alcohol, pornography, cigarettes, shoplifting, hobbies, conflict, religion, television, sugar, romance, exercise, money, material things, video games, working, approval, excitement, relationships, gambling, clothing, food, political views, your own thinking, control, anger, capitalism, socialism, conservatism, liberalism, shopping, plastic surgery, binging of any type, risky behaviors, pain, internet, cell phones, safety, security, the status quo, self-esteem, worth, validation, narcissism, power, and any other object or process that you feel you need or cannot live without!

They say that money doesn't buy happiness, but money doesn't buy you freedom either unless you are literally being held hostage with a ransom attached. I don't think we see how we are being held hostage when we are imprisoned by our dependency on any of the things I listed above as addictions.

For the record, I am not condemning any of the items on the list, for I believe there are two sides of everything. I am saying that if you need any of the above list to be happy, feel whole, or fill the hole within, there is a good chance that you have a dependency issue that might be bordering on an addiction.

The *Diagnostic and Statistical Manual of Mental Disorders*, Fifth Edition (DSM-5), describes an addiction as any disorder where impulses cannot be resisted.

We all have attachments in our lives that we believe we need. Indulging may bring a feeling of excitement. Spending may give us a temporary buzz and we are temporarily happy. The bigger the price tag, the longer the buzz, and yet it is still temporary. The length of time is also dependent on just how big a hole you're trying to fill.

Indulging is a way to numb out. It is a way to not have to face ourselves or an incredibly unpleasant situation. The avoidance causes us to numb out because we don't want to feel anything.

A mentor of mine, Jim Dethmer, once said that when you break off the antenna you use to feel so you do not feel bad, it is the same antenna that feels any and all feelings, even the good ones. The end result is that you just don't feel at all.

This desire to not feel creates a need to numb out more and more of the substance, process, or behavior to suppress the bad feelings and keep them from rising to the surface. Unfortunately, the feelings are there, and they do not go away. You must face them head on. You cannot numb them away.

CHAPTER 26
EXTRAORDINARY FREEDOM - PART II

> *I truly believe that the Twelve Step program (also known as Alcoholics Anonymous or AA) will go down in history as America's greatest and unique contribution to the history of spirituality.*
>
> **Richard Rohr**

BREAKING FREE – AWARENESS

I'm sure at this point you would like a surefire three-step process for breaking free. I don't have one for you.

What I do have is a short, reflective process to help you become more aware of areas that might be holding you prisoner. It is my hope that these will lead you to the place you've known you needed to go but have been afraid.

Place a check next to one or more of the items on the list where you feel you spend way too much time or would like to break free from, regardless of how much or how little.

List of Dependencies:

- ☐ Drugs
- ☐ Alcohol
- ☐ Pornography
- ☐ Cigarettes
- ☐ Shoplifting
- ☐ Hobbies
- ☐ Conflict
- ☐ Religion
- ☐ Television
- ☐ Sugar
- ☐ Romance
- ☐ Exercise
- ☐ Money
- ☐ Material things
- ☐ Video Games
- ☐ Work
- ☐ Approval
- ☐ Excitement
- ☐ Relationships
- ☐ Gambling
- ☐ Safety
- ☐ Security
- ☐ Status quo
- ☐ Self-esteem,
- ☐ Food
- ☐ Political Views
- ☐ Your Own Thinking
- ☐ Control
- ☐ Anger
- ☐ Capitalism
- ☐ Socialism
- ☐ Conservativism
- ☐ Liberalism
- ☐ Shopping
- ☐ Plastic Surgery
- ☐ Binging
- ☐ Risky Behaviors
- ☐ Pain
- ☐ Internet
- ☐ Social Media
- ☐ Cell Phone
- ☐ Clothing
- ☐ Food
- ☐ Self-worth (from external factors)
- ☐ Validation
- ☐ Narcissism
- ☐ Power
- ☐ _____

BREAKING FREE – QUESTIONS

In the end, you are the only person who can honestly determine your current state of freedom or imprisonment. You are the only person who can break yourself free from your dependencies.

Each question is directed toward the items you checked in the previous section.

TWELVE QUESTIONS TO DETERMINE YOUR LEVEL OF DEPENDENCY

1. Can you remember the last time you didn't act upon, think about, interact with, discuss, or crave this (these) items?
2. When you get stressed out, get bored, get angry, get depressed, want to escape, reward yourself, numb out, run away, or do not feel, do you reach out to any of these items to get relief?
3. Has your need for this item negatively affected your life, socially, financially, relationally, physically, mentally, or in any way?
4. Have you tried to give up any of the items or tried to control how much you use them and have been unable?
5. Have friends or family mentioned that you spend too much time or energy on this behavior?
6. Have you used this behavior to inflate your sense of self or to belittle others?
7. Does the buzz you get seem to have worn off or diminished?
8. Do you get anxious, upset, agitated, or uncomfortable if you are unable to interact with or use this item?
9. Do you find yourself thinking about or spending time wondering about the next time you have an opportunity to interact with this item?
10. Do you find yourself spending countless hours interacting with this item or losing track of time while engaged in it?
11. Do you find yourself spending more and more time engaged with this behavior?
12. Do you wish to be free from the substance, behavior, or process?

CHAPTER 26

DECIDING ON THE NEXT STEP

Addiction or dependency can be as simple as becoming aware of a behavior or mindset and making the necessary changes to let go and be more free. For example, if you cut down the amount of time you spend watching television and replace it with something more productive that moves you closer to your goals or objectives. It can be as simple as stating the new behaviors and monitoring your progress. I find at times that having an accountability partner to check in with, track your change, and give you a few pats on the back can be very helpful. On the other end of the spectrum, addiction and dependency can be life-threatening as in the case of substance abuse.

There are so many resources available depending on your level of dependency. The old stereotypes about addiction being only about substance abuse has changed dramatically since the founding of Alcoholics Anonymous by Dr. Bob Smith and Bill Wilson back in Akron, OH in 1935.

For many, the wide range and availability of twelve-step programs have proven to be invaluable. It is not simply a way to free yourself of addiction but a process to free yourself from the underlying beliefs, behaviors, and underlying unmet needs that typically drive the addiction or the dependency. You needn't be a substance abuser to find a program to help.

That said, twelve-step programs are not for everyone. As we learn more about human behavior, we learn more about the inexplicable ways we human beings learn to cope. As the world keeps changing, so do we.

The study of the human brain keeps expanding at an extraordinary rate. The science of neuro plasticity is changing our understanding of human behavior and what we are capable of achieving.

If we are to advance and become the very best version of ourselves, we must clear away the self-imposed obstacles we have placed in our pathway. It isn't to judge and blame ourselves or others for their existence. Most of us placed these obstacles there out of a means to protect our fragile sense of self or to prevent our wounds from being reopened.

The path to living an extraordinary life is a path that leads us to the best version of ourselves. It lies behind the facades, masks, and egocentric thinking that keeps us imprisoned. It is the freedom to be who we are, just as we are, knowing that we are loved and accepted without having to try to be someone else. There is an immense freedom in this mindset, and no one can ever take that away from you. That is what it means to be truly free!

Being truly free means that you are free wherever you go and whomever you are with. Whether you are surrounded by one or one-hundred people or are completely alone with just yourself and your thoughts. Some folks find either of these choices quite daunting.

In a world that continually bombards you with ads and other means to distract or to grab your attention, I find solitude is an extremely difficult thing to achieve.

CHAPTER 27
EXTRAORDINARY SOLITUDE

The reason I was uncomfortable with solitude,

was because I wasn't comfortable with myself.

Joe Contrera

Over the course of many years, I have concluded that there is a quantum difference between being alone and being lonely. This contrast has been spoken and written about many times before, but until you actually experience the difference, you cannot speak to it with any sense of credibility, wisdom, or experience. You could only parrot what others have said or experienced.

For a good part of my life, I was lonely. Because of my extroverted personality, I spent very little time alone because it felt like punishment or being banished to solitary confinement. So, I avoided it at all costs and was constantly surrounding myself with people and things to do or places to go. Even when I was a young child, my mother would ask me, "Don't you ever spend time alone?" I thought to myself, "Why on God's green Earth would I want to be alone when I can be with my friends?"

It took many years, but eventually, I realized the importance of spending time alone. It was one of the hardest things I have had to do, but I came to a tipping point because it was time to reassess and do what I had dreaded for years…be alone.

It was Saturday, February 8 and I was sitting in a restaurant on a date with an absolutely beautiful woman with whom I had absolutely no mental, emotional, or spiritual connection. I thought to myself, "What the hell am I doing? I am not even a bit interested in her."

It was as if I would have rather been with somebody, *anybody*, than to be alone on a Saturday night. It was shortly after that moment, after reflecting on my life, that I realized the constant in every failed relationship was *me*! I was at the scene of the crime in every situation. I made the decision that this was going to stop right then and there! So I decided to swear off dating for a minimum of one year and committed myself to solitude on a much grander scale.

A LITTLE HELP?

Sometimes life unfolds perfectly, in a way that couldn't be scripted any better if I had written it myself. The following month in March, the Covid-19 pandemic was beginning to spread quickly and most of us were forced into isolation.

In the beginning, time alone was a struggle, so I spent way too much time eating, drinking, and binge-watching my way through the initial boredom. After about ninety-days, I realized that I needed to recalibrate my goals and get myself back on track. It wasn't just my business goals but mental, spiritual, physical, and emotional goals as well. All these changes were good, but something was telling me that I had to go even deeper.

Later that year, I sold my house in Phoenix, Arizona and moved two hours north to Prescott. I halved the square footage of my home because I realized that a good part of my identity was wrapped up in the size of my house and my toys. So I unloaded a ton of furniture and "stuff" that I had grown very attached to over the years. I bought a home on a heavily-wooded lot surrounded by tons of deer, javelina, and mountain lions. I had dabbled with spending time alone on and off over the years but never to this magnitude. This was going to require a great deal of self-reflection, growth, and (gulp) solitude!

At first, I woke up in the mornings to see deer passing through the property. I set up bird feeders and a giant water trough for the wildlife. I took online courses and worked on writing this very book while continuing to coach my clients. Knowing others were being quarantined also made it a bit easier to accept. But as time passed and one weekend melted into the next, things became extremely challenging, and I started bouncing between the joyful feeling of solitude and the sadness and pain of feeling utterly alone.

AN EPIPHANY

One day as I sat in my chair reading, writing, and meditating, I had an epiphany of sorts. I finally learned what all those years of avoiding solitude was wanting to teach me:

> *"The reason I was uncomfortable with solitude, was because I wasn't comfortable with myself."*

I'M FINE

For years I thought I was just fine. Whenever issues arose, I dealt with them whether that required a tough conversation with myself or someone else. At times I would reach out to others for help to work through an issue, but for the most part, I believed I was comfortable with whom I was as a person.

It wasn't until I pushed myself far beyond my comfort zone and let go of the things that defined me externally that I realized just how much this underlying issue of not wanting to be alone was creating problems in so many other areas of my life.

Spending time alone can be easy if you numb out with food, alcohol, social media, and/or television. It becomes extremely challenging when you sit back, read, and reflect or just sit alone in contemplation. However, there is something very freeing when you cut yourself loose from all those distractions and come to the realization that you are just fine all by yourself.

YOU COMPLETE ME

There is a moment in the movie *Jerry Maguire* where Tom Cruise is standing in the living room of his almost ex-wife, played by Renee Zellweger, where he utters the second-most remembered line from the entire movie, "You complete me." That line is then followed by the first-most remembered line from the movie, "Shut up. You had me at hello." They embrace, they fall back in love, and of course, they live happily-ever-after, just like all the other fairy tale endings.

This is the story so many of us are taught from a very young age. All the talk about one's promised other-half, better-half, heart's desire, my love, the one, soulmate, true love, and all the other crap peddled in the name of love that should be labeled for what it is…codependency!

You must be comfortable with yourself before you can be comfortable with someone else. You must bring a whole person into a relationship, not half of person, expecting the other person to complete you and meet all your needs.

COMPLETE YOURSELF

Until I was willing to let go of the need for a significant other, partner, spouse, etc., so I could become a whole person on my own, I was never going to be a great partner for anyone.

Learning to be alone and to reflect on yourself, your life, your purpose, who you are, why you are here, what you want, is essential to becoming a whole person. And when you become a whole person, you realize that you can be comfortable being alone with yourself.

Taking time to experience extraordinary solitude can allow you to look deeply into those areas of your life that are uncomfortable and help you find the doorway to freedom. They represent the pathway toward taking the next big step to living an extraordinary life regardless of which aspect of your life needs to be examined. In solitude, you will uncover the things that have been holding you back for years.

Extraordinary solitude doesn't mean you divorce your spouse, break up with your partner, abandon your children, go on a three-month sabbatical, or take a pilgrimage to Mecca. It simply means taking time to be alone, to sit and be with yourself, whether in meditation, contemplative prayer, or whatever other path you choose to get you feeling comfortable being alone with yourself.

It is a foundational process that will take you closer toward living the life you have always wanted…an extraordinary life.

CHAPTER 28
AN EXTRAORDINARY LIFE: IS IT YOURS?

Tell me I've led a good life...tell me I am a good man!
From the Movie Saving Private Ryan

Movies have always been a way for me to connect to my emotions. There has always been a smorgasbord of movies in my library that I have watched so many times that I know the actors' lines by heart. *Awakenings, Gladiator, When Harry Met Sally, Drop-Dead Fred, Braveheart, About Last Night, Synchronicity,* the *Rocky* series (yes, all of them except for *Rocky V*) the *Rambo* series, *An Affair to Remember (original version),* and of course *The Godfather (I & II).*

There are other movies I have seen just a few times. *Schindler's List, Leaving Las Vegas, 8MM,* and *Saving Private Ryan* would be titles that fall into this category. These are the ones that leave a sick feeling in the pit of my stomach for various reasons, whether it is the sheer evil that is portrayed in those films, the total devaluing of a human life, or an explicit, in-your-face reminder of the painful and tragic side of being human.

The opening war scene of *Saving Private Ryan* and the closing cemetery scene are bookends that speak to two diametrically-opposed views about life. Both have impacted me in an emotionally-powerful way.

CHAPTER 28

A TRIP BACK IN TIME

The movie begins with an old man and his family walking through the cemetery in Normandy France. If you have never been there, the sheer number of gravesites is so overwhelming that you can't not be emotionally impacted at the magnitude of war in some way.

As he walks, his family following closely behind him, he turns and goes down a row of white stone gravesites until he finds the one he is looking for. It is just one of the 9,386 graves of those who lost their lives storming the beaches of Normandy and the ensuing operations.

The old man is so overwhelmed by emotion that he falls to his knees. His family rushes to his side as the camera zooms in on his face before you are whisked back in time, some fifty-three years earlier to the largest amphibious landing of men in the history of war—Operation Overlord.

D-DAY

It is June 6, 1945, D-day, and Allied Forces are landing on the shores of France. Literally thousands of men are assaulting the shore directly into enemy machine-gun fire and mortars. Bullets are whizzing in every direction, killing men in the water and on the beach. Some do not even make it off their landing craft. It is a scene of pure chaos and horror.

A close friend of mine whose father had been there asked him if the movie gave a realistic perspective of what took place that day. He replied, "It wasn't even close, it was so much worse!"

Watching human beings being shredded and torn apart makes the value of a human life appear to be meaningless. Regardless of the why or the intention, D-day, like Vietnam and many wars, seems to be a numbers game. The more bodies you throw at something, the higher the probability of success, sometimes.

Eventually, the Allies succeed after the extraordinary courage of the men who fought on that day and throughout the war. I want to be very careful here in stating that I am not in any way diminishing the sacrifices those men made on that day, in that war, or in any other war. We are free because of the sacrifices others have made so we can enjoy the freedoms we have.

However, I am looking at the way we now trivialize war, violence, and the value of a human life. The media, Hollywood, and video-game makers have taken killing and violence to a whole new level. These video games that young people engage in for hours have created a numbness to the reality of violence and the killing of another human being.

How can you live an extraordinary life if you don't value life? How can you live an extraordinary life if those who died defending your freedom are not respected, appreciated, or remembered? It is like so many things in life, a paradox.

At the other end of the spectrum, we have become oversensitive to the presence of statues, words, and labels that even slightly offend anyone who raises an objection.

There are those who believe if you don't want to take down a statue of a president who had slaves, you are a racist. However, if I leave the protest, go home, fire up my Xbox and simulate shooting a prostitute with a 9MM Glock because I didn't want to pay her, that's just perfectly fine.

THE STORY

Once past the opening scene of *Saving Private Ryan*, the movie progresses through the story about four brothers—three who are killed on D-day. The remaining brother is to be found and returned home, and his name is Private James Ryan, played by a young Matt Damon.

Tom Hanks plays Lt. John Miller, the man in charge of a small company of soldiers assigned to find him and return him home. As the story unfolds, this small group of soldiers search the French countryside and come across various encounters with the enemy. You learn to develop a liking for each member of the team in different ways, which adds to the sadness as they are killed in various engagements with the enemy.

Eventually, they find Private Ryan, who is now a part of a small group left to defend a bridge in a small French town that has been ravaged by the war. Wanting to grab Ryan and leave before the Germans arrive, Ryan refuses to abandon his fellow soldiers. The decision is made to combine forces and defend the town, and more importantly, to prevent the Germans from crossing the bridge. The order: Defend the bridge or blow it up.

Throughout the movie, a little of each actor's character and story is revealed. It is just enough so that you have some emotional connection to each of them. When the final battle scene unfolds, their deaths hit you in a much more personal way, and you now experience the impact of their deaths in a much deeper way. It is the antithesis of the opening battle.

The entire company of men are killed. Three men remain, and Private Ryan is one of them. Tom Hanks is mortally wounded in his attempt to blow up the bridge, and he is the last resort. He is being fired upon, and as he fires his pistol at the explosives wired to the bridge, a P-51 Mustang screams overhead and attacks the Germans.

Ryan runs to Hanks as he lies there dying, and Hanks whispers something to him. You hear the words, "Earn this! Earn this, James!"

In other words, never forget that men died so that you could have a life. Don't waste your life!

AN EXTRAORDINARY BURDEN

Fast forward fifty-three years, and an aged Private James Ryan is down on one knee in front of the tombstone of Capt. John Miller. His family, wife, kids, and grandchildren are slightly blurred in the background behind him. He says, "Every day, I think about what you said to me that day on the bridge. I tried to live my life the best I could. I hope that was enough. I hope that at least in your eyes, I earned what all of you did for me."

He stands back up as his wife approaches him. "Captain John Miller," she says. He turns to her and says, "Tell me I've led a good life. Tell me I am a good man!"

For fifty-three years since that day on the bridge, Private James Ryan has been living with the question of whether he lived a life worth living in the eyes of a man he barely knew, but who sacrificed his life so Private James Ryan could live.

Imagine the weight, the burden, and the guilt of judging yourself everyday as to whether you were worthy or enough?

AM I ENOUGH?

I think that many of us bump against this same question, albeit in a less dramatic way. I believe that question is something so many people try to answer on a daily basis, sometimes consciously, and sometimes unconsciously. It originates in our desire to prove our sense of self-worth and value.

The desire to prove our self-worth and value shows up in a multitude of ways:

- An excessive striving for success.
- Climbing the corporate ladder.
- Materialism and the need for more things or money.
- Desperately seeking and searching to be loved or made whole through someone other than yourself.
- Addictions and substances we use to fill the hole and mask our emotions or feelings of inadequacy.

When we live our lives driven by a burden of guilt, shame, or to meet the expectations of others, we miss out on the opportunity to live an ex-

CHAPTER 28

traordinary life where we are free to create our version of extraordinary. While it may make for an extraordinary movie, I am not sure it fulfills the point I am trying to make and the core message of this book, yet we must be able to step back and see both sides of the story. We must be able to embrace both life and death.

CHAPTER 29
AN EXTRAORDINARY LIFE - FOR REAL

Somebody should tell us, right at the start of our lives, that we are dying. Then we might live life to the limit, every minute of every day. Do it! I say. Whatever you want to do, do it now! There are only so many tomorrows.

Pope Paul VI

WAIT FOR IT?

There has been much written about the end of life. Many people have shared what they believe happens at the end of a person's life. We guess, we theorize, but the reality of what actually happens is unknown.

I believe the most realistic writing on this topic comes from what hospice nurses have shared about what they see happening when people in their care are nearing death.

It is well known that most people on their death beds have at least one or two regrets. Most of the regrets have to do with being truer to themselves, not working so hard, being more courageous in some area of their life, or some regret regarding relationships, forgiveness, or being more loving.

We've read or heard about all these things over the course of our lives, but we still live life as if that day will never come.

Why is it that so many of us wait till we get to the end of our lives, and only *then* reflect on how we lived our life: the regrets we have, the mistakes we made, the things that bring us happiness, the things we wish we had done more or less, and whether or not we have led a good life or were a good person? Why is it that some of us overestimate our goodness while many of us underestimate it?

REFLECTIONS ON A LIFE

I was sitting in Parma Community Hospital. Rose Amelia Adornetto Contrera, my ninety-one-year-old mother, was sleeping next to me in her hospital bed as I was typing these words. She was hospitalized again, this time with double pneumonia. I came home four days earlier because we were not sure if she was going to survive this last trauma.

I was here a week and a half earlier to visit her for Mother's Day. I had not seen her for a year and a half because of Covid. Since November of 2020, she had been hospitalized four times, Thanksgiving, Christmas, Easter and shortly after Mother's Day.

Over the course of the last four days, we have been reminiscing about her life and our life together. To say my mother is an extraordinary woman who has led an extraordinary life would be an understatement in my eyes. If you asked her if she had an extraordinary life, she would tell you emphatically *no*! She would tell you she had a good life and was blessed with family and friends.

In many areas of her life, she pushed beyond what was safe, comfortable, and known.

She never graduated high school or finished her GED, even though she attempted to later in life. At the age of sixteen, while in high school, she was hospitalized as a result of testing positive for Tuberculosis and placed on an iron lung. This disease would subtlety lurk in the background her entire life and would be the eventual cause of her death.

During our time together, she shared a story I had never heard. She told me that when she was laying in that hospital bed at the age of sixteen, she prayed to God that if he needed her to take care of someone or something, she would accept and unconditionally love whomever he would send her. Her words, not mine. At that time, she recalled being momentarily struck with a sharp pain in her chest.

AN ANSWERED PRAYER

She gave birth to three boys, one who was developmentally challenged and created many incredibly challenging situations throughout her life. For many years, the Parma Police were regular visitors at our home, but never once did she or my father ever consider putting him in a home or institution, even though this was the norm for many kids like him in those days. To her, he was not broken, nor was he ever to be hidden in the background. He was always at the forefront of our family. For her, he was nothing other than a blessing from God and an answer to a prayer from years earlier.

She is one of the most determined women I have ever known. She was one headstrong lady. She never stopped learning, trying new things, or pushing her limits. Whether it was driving one-handed and holding on to my brother Billy with the other when the door of the car flew open on the highway (he probably opened it), learning to play golf late in life so she could play every Tuesday morning in a league, playing Bocce every Wednesday evenings, or learning to bowl so she could play every Friday morning, she pushed herself outside of her comfort zones in many areas of her life.

In 1983, she traveled by herself with a group to Bosnia and Herzegovina to the small town of Medjugorje on a Catholic pilgrimage because as she said, "I was called to go there!" She would tell you the story of climbing Apparition Hill, where the Virgin Mary had allegedly appeared in 1981, if you asked. Of course, this had nothing to do with Mom wanting to visit. Even though the archaic and patriarchal Catholic Church does not condone or acknowledge Medjugorje (conventional wisdom), she knew deep in her heart—damn well why she went—what she saw and what she knew was the truth, her truth (alternative wisdom).

Her faith was a driving force in her life and would be up until her very last breath. Many of my clients would call and ask for her to pray for them or someone in their family. The most famous four words whenever anyone called to ask for prayers were, "I'll call the nuns!" Mom was the go-to prayer warrior whenever my clients were faced with life's obstacles and challenges.

Ironically, when Mom was ill and nearing the end of her life, I received a call from one of my clients—Jack Hirschmann and his wife Laura whom Mom had called the nuns for a few times. They were wanting the phone number of the nuns of St. Joseph in Rocky River, Ohio, so they could call and have prayers said for my mom. Her faith influenced the lives of so many people that I cannot even begin to count.

ROSIE THE RIVETER

I remember a trip home from college after my sophomore year. I walked into the house one Friday afternoon, plunked my duffle bag of clothes on the landing, and shouted out, "Mom, I'm home!" I heard her down in the basement shouting, "I'm down here!"

As I walked down the stairs, I saw my mother bent over the laundry sink sporting a pair of plastic safety glasses. In one hand is a lit blow torch, and in the other hand is a coil of solder! She is burning through the solder at an incredibly fast rate, and it is dripping all over the sink, the pipe, and the wall. She had no idea what she was doing but that would never stop her from pushing outside of her limits. The expression on her face was of sheer determination. It was as if she were Rosie the Riveter working on the wing of a B-52 bomber during World War II that would bomb the enemy!

I asked her, "What the hell are you doing?" She replied, "I am fixing the pipe. There, that ought to do it!" She shut off the torch, took off her glasses, put down the solder, and gave me a hug. She then proceeded to turn on the faucet as water sprayed all over her for the third time. Most people would've quit, but not my mom. She wiped off the pipe, fired up the torch, and went right back at it as if it were the first time.

A DIFFERENT KIND OF EXTRAORDINARY

After a week in the hospital, Rosie began her recovery in Mt. Alverna Nursing Home. Each day she pushed herself to do one more exercise than she was asked to do and one more repetition in occupational therapy than required. Even at the age of ninety-one years, she continued to go beyond what was comfortable and easy.

One day I walked into to visit her as she was bending over in her wheelchair, teaching the nurse the easiest way to put on compression hose! The nurse was entranced so much in my mom's words that she didn't even know I'd entered the room. You just can't make this stuff up!

When you are clear about your purpose, you do whatever you must to accomplish it. Mom was crystal clear about what she deemed to be her purpose, and she never wavered. In her mind, God had given her a purpose—someone to watch over—and she would fight like hell to make sure she would fulfill her promise to the last breath of her life.

I mentioned earlier that as we progress through life, the challenges and decisions we are faced with change. Sometimes, the decisions we face are slow in coming, sometimes they are dramatic, and sometimes they happen overnight.

Less than four weeks later, she awoke at 5:30 a.m. and went to the bathroom unattended where she became unconscious while experiencing a stroke. She found the strength to pull the emergency chain before she went unconscious. She was found unresponsive on the bathroom floor and rushed to the hospital.

On my next visit, I sat watching her struggle to do the simplest of things. She could barely hold her head up and she could not speak, no matter how hard she tried. Her right side was paralyzed, and she was unable to walk or feed herself. The simplest things in life, such as feeding herself or sitting up, were impossible for her at that time.

NEVER STOP

Over the course of the next few weeks, we saw glimpses of recovery. She might utter a singular word or a four-word sentence, pushing herself to try a little more every day. One day after a few steps backward, we were surprised when her caregiver Debbie sent us a video. While seated upright in her reclining wheelchair, she reached for her spoon and began to feed herself. All the things that she once had done so effortlessly, overnight required tremendous acts of courage and determination. Her definition of being extraordinary changed overnight!

The Serenity Prayer reminds us to accept those things that we cannot change, the courage to change the things we can, and the wisdom to know the difference. My hope is that you will use Mom's story as a reminder to change those areas of your life where you can, long before it becomes an area you cannot, and you must simply accept it as it is in that moment!

WE ALL HAVE BLIND SPOTS

Rosie pushed beyond her comfort zone in several areas of her life. When it came to her faith, she remained steadfast and unbending, even in the face of cold-hard facts.

When scandals rocked the Catholic Church, she remained steadfast and true. Never once did she condemn the church, the pope, or any of the priests. It was as if acknowledging the truth would cause the entire foundation of her life to crumble and disappear. Along with it, she would lose her safety, security, and comfort.

I guess this confirms what Voltaire said, "The human brain is a complex organ with the wonderful power of enabling man to find reasons for continuing to believe whatever it is that he wants to believe."

Of course, like all of us, there were other beliefs she held on to that prevented her from moving beyond that stuck place, such as the intense devotion to her mother and some of the fear-based beliefs that were imprinted upon her that lived inside of her for years. She held the belief that she wasn't smart enough because she never graduated high school or received her GED. She remembered events where she felt she had been wronged. I think this was one of the reasons three of her favorite movies were *The Sound of Music, Somewhere in Time,* and *Death Wish II*.

During these days of sitting by her bedside, I asked her whether she thought she was going to heaven. Sadly, she replied, "Oh no, you have to be really good in order to get to heaven. I didn't pray enough to get to heaven!" (This, even though she prayed more for others than any other woman I have ever known except for Mother Theresa).

Most of all, the one that saddens me the most was the internal belief that she carried her entire life. It was the belief that she had to earn the love of God and others through her actions, prayers, and good works.

In many ways, as I reflect on my mom's life, I believe it was nothing short of extraordinary. In other ways, I wondered what might have been had she been able to let go and move beyond some of those old beliefs that held her back, striving to be enough, instead of just knowing that she was.

Each and every day, you are faced with a thousand decisions. Some are trivial and trite, like what to have for breakfast, watch on tv, etc.

Then there are those decisions that determine or alter the course of your life, like knowing which choice to make, when to make it, and which action to take when faced with these life altering choices?

Well, that is the trillion-dollar question, isn't it?

CHAPTER 29

A STORY OF EXTRAORDINARY LOVE

As I mentioned previously, at the age of sixteen, my mom had asked God for someone to take care of and her prayer was answered when she and my father were blessed with my brother Billy. Yes, you can say that she was blessed with all of us, but there was a special bond between her and Billy. There is a myth about folks who are developmentally challenged. Remember, a myth has an essence of truth about it versus a fantasy (like Santa Claus) that does not. Some folks believe that developmentally-challenged folks are the result of a god and a human coming to together and giving birth to a human.

At the very end of her life, when it appeared she was holding onto something or someone, my brother Billy went into her room and told her, "Mom, I love you. I am going to be okay. You can go."

Twenty minutes later, she was gone.

To me, I cannot write, nor have I experienced a greater story of love. It encompasses every possible facet of love, love of God, love of self, love of family, and love of life…an extraordinary love woven into an extraordinary life.

CHAPTER 30
WHAT MAKES UP AN EXTRAORDINARY LIFE

An extraordinary life isn't a place where you finally arrive. It isn't a destination. It is a collection of thousands and thousands of decisions you make throughout your life. It isn't a matter of good or bad, or right or wrong! It is about the decisions you make each time you decide to step beyond what is common, known, safe, secure, and comfortable.

Joe Contrera

I WANT ABSOLUTES

We humans make more than 35,000 decisions per day. Over the course of a year that is roughly 12,775,000 decisions every year. It is impossible to always know exactly what to hold onto or when to let go, when to sit or to move, whether to take the narrow path to the left or the wide path to the right. How we can guarantee we always will make the right decision is the hundred-trillion-dollar question.

We would all love the manual, the book, or authority figure who can tell us with no uncertain terms that we should choose A, B, or C. Some of us even kid ourselves into believing that we can find absolutes in the pope, the government, our parents, some guru, or a book just like this one. It simply isn't the truth. If you believe that, then you are probably stuck in a mindset that is preventing you from moving forward.

The truth is that no one can determine for you which decisions you should make. They can only project their own beliefs and thoughts onto you and your situation, which makes this somewhat frustrating and scary.

The truth is most of us would rather abdicate that responsibility to someone else. We want to know we are making the right decision because we don't want to experience the pain or regret of making the wrong one. We want absolutes to feel comfortable, safe, and secure.

EMBRACING A BIGGER STORY

If we want to live an extraordinary life, we must embrace the bigger, broader, and wider story, which includes the undeniable truth that life is filled with uncertainty and pain we cannot avoid. We must learn to navigate between two sides of everything while not excluding anything. You simply make the best decision you can at that exact moment in time and know there is nothing all good or all bad, all black or all white, or all right or all wrong. That is a very dualistic exclusionary mindset, as said many times before, and limits your ability to grow.

When, not if, you choose a path that doesn't end up creating the results you expected, wished for, or wanted, you simply shift directions, decide differently, and take an action to alter your course. It is that simple.

LIVING IN REGRET

I have a friend who lives in a world of regret. She constantly goes back in time and rehashes decisions she made stating she should have chosen differently. It could be a decision she made a day, week, month, or even twenty-years ago that she regrets. She lives in the past, wishing for a better future and missing out on the beauty of the present. It is as if the black clouds of would have, should have, or could have pour rain on her daily. While it may be a defense mechanism to keep her stuck and prevent her from moving forward, it is a world filled with a false sense of comfort and security that she has become quite accustomed. I wonder if this is what Pink Floyd meant by the song entitled, *Comfortably Numb*.

The secret to living an extraordinary life is knowing that you are going to make mistakes, *but*—and that is a very big "but"—every second of every moment, every hour, every day, every month, or every year, you can choose differently. You can choose to push forward and step outside of your comfort zone and choose to be extraordinary. As we discussed in Chapter 12 regarding Tom Peters and becoming world-class, you just have to decide.

A MILLION DECISIONS, A MILLION MOMENTS

You see, it is the accumulation of all those decisions that you make in all of those 36,792,000 or more moments over the course of your life that will determine the level of extraordinariness you achieve, whether you choose to play it safe or decide consistently to push yourself outside of what you know to be common, known, secure, and comfortable.

No one can decide whether you are living an extraordinary life but you. Never let anyone hold that power over you or take it away from you. Never, ever give your power away!

As I was searching for ways to bring this book to a close, I reached out to a very dear friend and colleague, Barry Zweibel. I was struggling immensely, and nothing I wrote or rewrote no matter how many times was capturing what I intended to say.

Barry and I have known each other for over twenty years, and he has a way of asking me incredible questions that help me gain clarity on my thoughts and ideas so I can transform them into words. As we brainstormed ideas, he asked me a question that hit me like a 4 by 4 board to

CHAPTER 30

the side of the head, "Joe, are *you* living an extraordinary life?" My ego wanted to blurt out, "Of course I am. I'm writing a book about it!"

However, it was in that exact moment in time that I realized that, in several areas in my life, I was pushing beyond the comfort, into the fear, and into the unknown, but there were a few other areas that I *still* needed to work on. These were areas where I had created a nice little fortress where I could protect my thinking and old beliefs that were no longer serving me. In fact, they were holding me back.

The epiphany—or wake-up call, skies parting, and a voice coming down from heaven, whatever you want to call it—was this: In my striving and determination to write an end-all, save-all book that would change your life, I realized there were still a few areas in my own life I needed to change.

The desire to live an extraordinary life is an ongoing, never-ending accumulation of the choices I make in each and every moment of my life. For me, when I get to the end of my life, I hope I can honestly say, "I am empty, I left it all on the table. I chose to step outside of my fears so many times and in so many more ways than when I let my fears hold me back." I will then be content, knowing for myself, I lived an extraordinary life.

My path has had its share of mistakes, slips, falls, and times of being quite lost. I think some of us want or expect our path to be without any of those things—a painless path. I don't think that is humanly possible.

The stories you tell of yourself are simply stories, and our lives seem to be made up of a collection of stories—some happy, some sad, some joy-filled, and others not so much. Then there are the stories other people tell about us when we're not there or after we are gone. That is and will be your legacy!

It is my greatest wish that you leave behind an extraordinary legacy knowing that you lived an extraordinary life. In some small way, I hope this book and these thoughts gave you a glimpse and insight into the best version of you, and in some small way, I hope it helped you get there!

EPILOGUE

So much has changed since I first started writing this book toward the tail end of 2019. A world-wide pandemic basically shut down life as we knew it and created a new normal of quarantining, shortages, and isolation.

At the same time, I uprooted my life and moved to a more rural community two hours from everyone and everything I knew for the past seventeen years of my life.

I stopped the roller coaster ride I was on and took a year and a half away from relationships and dating. For the first time in my life, I was alone for an extended length of time. I was away from my family for a year and a half, longer than I had ever experienced in my entire life. Prior to the pandemic, I had never gone longer than five months between visits and never missed consecutive holidays.

It was a time of extreme isolation and extreme growth. I am not the same person who started writing this book nearly two years ago, and this is not the book I intended to write. Sometimes what we set out to do isn't what results from our intentions or our actions.

The world is slowly coming back to life. It is a time of reorder as we find ourselves attempting to navigate this new normal. It will require strength, hope, and an unshakable belief that we are evolving into something new, something better, and a better version of ourselves as a race.

It is easy to get pulled down into the muck of politics, negativity, mud-slinging, and hatred that seems to be running rampant in our world. This

CHAPTER 30

is magnified by the various forms of media that want to divide and split us into fractions so they can sell more ads.

Abraham Lincoln said, "A nation divided against itself cannot stand."

You must first know what you stand for before you can take a stand for yourself. You can allow fear, hatred, and self-centeredness to be the rock upon which you stand. You can make yourself right and others wrong as you stand in groups of like-minded people, making enemies of anyone with whom you disagree, and we will fall as a nation!

The other choice is to go outside of the self-limiting beliefs we have about ourselves and each other. We can choose to include and seek out our similarities rather than our differences. We can understand that we are not many races, but one race—the human race. In doing so, we can create a world that is extraordinary.

APPENDIX - Q & A

A good portion of your intro focused on looking within to become a better leader at work. What if you don't want to be a leader at work? You simply want to be a better spouse, parent, or individual in your own life. Will your principles apply to this?

> The short answer is yes! Being extraordinary is more of a mindset than a leadership style. It is a way to approach change—a way to be. Obviously, how you navigate change determines your trajectory in life, whether you fight it, simply acknowledge it, fear it, or embrace it.

I feel as if I am living an extraordinary life now. How does this help me?

> Someone once said that if you are coasting, chances are you are going downhill. Similarly, Gandhi said that nothing in life is static. We are either moving forward or backward. Moving forward doesn't always mean we are taking action. It might mean that we are letting go of something to free us to move forward more easily. There is a natural cycle to life. It ebbs and flows, there is birth, and there is death. Life has a natural tendency to cause atrophy and entropy. Human beings tend to seek comfort and security. I guess if that is how you define an extraordinary life, then that is what it is for you. The whole idea of this book is to get you to look at those areas of your life where you are not living to your

potential, whether it is because you are holding yourself back or not realizing your full potential.

Does an 'Extraordinary Life' mean having everything you want, or being happy with where you are and who you are in your own life?

Living an extraordinary life doesn't mean you get everything you want. We humans want a lot of things, many of which we really don't need, especially if we are using those things to fill a hole. Living an extraordinary life doesn't necessarily mean being content with who you are and where you are in life either. It is all about pushing beyond our comfort zones and realizing our full potential. We seem to get easily lulled to sleep by external components: television, the media, fear, our need for safety and security, albeit a false sense of security. Expansion beyond that false sense of comfort and security is what drives us to live an extraordinary life.

What ideas do you have about getting those people who don't care, or are living mindlessly, to care or seek some help?

Ideas? Nothing really. It is usually pain that wakes people up to the possibility of something more. Most folks, however, fall back asleep after the pain goes away. Others mask the pain with busyness, drugs, alcohol, or some other addiction to numb it out. If people aren't ready or don't desire something more, to me, there is nothing that is going to change that. Better to let it go and move on from them, instead of expending energy to get them to do something they are not ready to do. It is a matter of trusting that the universe, God, consciousness, or whatever you want to label this life force, is in control and things are unfolding perfectly for that person, even if it is not what you think it should be!

When I realize my ego is running things, how can I help myself?

Great question! Some indicators that show your ego is running the show are getting upset, angry, disgruntled, comparing, excluding, judging, condemning, feeling the need to be better than or a step above others, or simply feeling the need to inflate your sense of self. I also believe that when we are beating ourselves up, condemning ourselves, feeling guilty, shameful, not good enough, or less than, that is also an indicator that our ego is working overtime. It is in those times that we need to surrender, let go, and remind ourselves of who we are and our purpose on earth—that we are brilliant, loved, and simply were reverting to an old tape or program that no longer serves us.

I want to be extraordinary. How will I know "I have made it?"

There is no external scale to measure your level of extraordinariness, only an internal one. When you ask yourself not if you're content but if you're stepping outside of what you find to be comfortable, safe, and secure in the various areas of your life laid out in the book, that is when you know you are approaching living an extraordinary life. It is a very personal thing, and the measurement is against your own limits, not by someone or something that is outside of you. I believe that is what makes this concept of living an extraordinary life so life-changing. You never really arrive at a destination because like life, is it an ever-changing, ever-evolving, for-life process, and we must learn to adapt to every phase. What we experience and how we experience life in our twenties are not what or how we experience it in our fifties. Our ability to respond is mentally and physically a bit more challenging the older we get. There is a natural path of atrophy after we reach a certain age, and you realize it when you come to realize that things like losing weight or getting in shape are so much easier when we are younger than when we hit a certain point in our development. It seems to happen somewhere between thirty and forty. Think about the gym or losing weight, and that will help you understand what I mean. It is then that we must work a bit harder to step outside of our comfort zones and move beyond them.

CHAPTER 30

What is my first step to achieving an extraordinary life?

Self-awareness is the first step. That means being open to the possibility that you are unconscious in a few areas of your life that need some self-reflection to change and to sustain that change throughout your life. It is as if once you wake up, it is difficult to fall back to sleep if you stay on the path. As I have pointed out in the early chapters of this book, there are a lot of folks who would prefer you to be asleep. The church, the government, and media of all types work tirelessly to lull you back into a state of unconsciousness.

What can I do daily to challenge myself to be extraordinary?

Look for areas where you can step beyond what you know, what is safe, and what is comfortable. For example, if you are an introvert, smile and say hello to folks at the grocery store. If you are an extrovert, instead of consistently blurting out your thoughts or emotions, keep silent, sit, and meditate because it is the opposite of what you typically do. It is a bit uncomfortable. Regularly ask yourself, "What would I do if I wasn't afraid? What small step could I take that would nudge me into an action or idea I have always wanted to take or implement?" These are just a few small steps you can take on a daily basis to challenge yourself to be even more extraordinary.

How can I lead others to become extraordinary?

Just like leading horses to water, you can lead them there and invite them to drink. However, if they are not thirsty, they will not drink. It is their choice, and it is up to them. In my previous book, *Extraordinary Results*, I spent a lot of time talking about leadership and the art of asking great questions. The idea is that you ask questions to shine a light on the obstacle that is stopping the other person from moving forward. Once they see the obstacle or the situation from a few different angles, they are more apt to find a solution or a way out of their dilemma. Aside from that, it is really up to them. Wanting people to succeed more than they want that for themselves is a slippery slope that many parents and leaders fall into.

If I choose to avoid negative people, does that make me *not* extraordinary?

I think the key here is to identify whether the negativity is a temporary obstacle in their life or if it is a way of life. We are all faced with obstacles or tough times along the way, but it is when being a victim or being constantly negative becomes a person's modus operandi that I believe it is best to stay away or limit your exposure. So no, for the record, I believe that makes you even more extraordinary, not less!

What is the end goal of an extraordinary life? Is it happiness, peace, contentment, self-satisfaction, a large salary or...?

I think it is whatever you decide it is. As I said before, living your extraordinary life is a very personal thing. The key is making sure you have a high-enough level of self-awareness and do enough self-reflection to make sure you are not kidding yourself into to believing everything is fine, life is good, and you are happy when you are not.

Is an extraordinary life a never-ending process? Is there an "end zone" in sight or do the "goalposts" keep moving?

As we age and pass through the various phases of life, things evolve. Our bodies change, and we hopefully have acquired more knowledge and experiences. As we continue moving forward, we will realize that in some ways what was outside our comfort zone years ago is easy and we will also find that somethings that were easy have become a challenge. So, for me, the end zone is knowing I never settled or stopped going outside of whatever was common, comfortable, known, and secure.

Can you still be an effective leader without being extraordinary?

> I can offer my subjective opinion on that. I think as a leader, how can you ask your people to keep growing and stretching if you settle for being ineffective and not extraordinary? Maybe the better question is do you want your people to be effective or extraordinary? Answer that one, and you will find your answer.

Is there a minimal place one needs to be mentally to take this on? By that I mean, are there personal prerequisites to prepare for this journey to extraordinary success?

> I think the only thing that would be a prerequisite is the willingness to take a long, honest, look at oneself. This will automatically cause a certain level of discomfort and if you're willing to do that, you are on your way to taking the first steps toward creating an extraordinary life. By the way, you reference extraordinary success. Success doesn't necessarily equate to happiness. I know some very successful people who are miserable because they lack purpose or a sense of significance.

Can someone who is really crappy change? I would argue that servant leadership can't be undertaken by someone who is selfish, arrogant, egotistical, etc.

> I agree that servant leadership is the anthesis of selfishness, arrogance, and ego. I think it is important to separate the crappy behavior from the person. Crappy behavior doesn't necessarily equal a crappy person. There is a saying in Alcoholics Anonymous—love the alcoholic, hate the disease. If an addict can change, why can't someone with crappy behavior change? Gandhi said, "Be the change you wish to see in the world." Maybe try changing how you view and treat this person and see what happens?

How does a parent instill those basic building blocks in their children for living an extraordinary life?

> Great question! Throughout the book I reference beliefs that we

get imprinted with from an early age. I think if we can teach kids about the reality of life, about love, about pain, adversity, joy, happiness, meaning the full spectrum of what life is, we are helping them immensely. Being a helicopter or lawn-mover parent and removing any adversity weakens them and doesn't prepare them for the real world. The truth is life can at times be extraordinary and at times be painful. You can't have one without the other!

Can lousy leaders become great leaders?

Of course, if they are willing to look at themselves and how they are negatively impacting their people. More times than not, in my experience it is an educational thing—meaning we do a poor job of selecting and educating our leaders. Usually we pick high-performing individual contributors and throw them in a leadership position without educating them on leadership or providing the tools they need to be successful. For a much more detailed explanation on this topic, pick up a copy of my last book entitled, *Extraordinary Results: Mastering the Art of Leading, Coaching & Influencing Others.*

RESOURCES

Abramson, Ashley. "Substance Use During the Pandemic." *America Psychological Association* 52, no 2 (2021): 22. https://www.apa.org/monitor/2021/03/substance-use-pandemic#:~:text=Overdoses%20have%20also%20spiked%20since,those%20same%20months%20in%202019.

Contrera, Joe. *Extraordinary Results: Mastering the Art of Leading, Coaching & Influencing Others.* Prescott, AZ: Alive @ Work Publishing, 2018.

Deutschman, Alan. *Change or Die: The Three Keys to Change at Work and in Life.* New York: Harper Business, 2007.

Bedrock Recovery Center. "Drug Use Statistics." https://bedrockrecoverycenter.com/drug-abuse-statistics/.

Herrig, Andrew. "Personal Finance Statistics 2021: Shocking Facts on Money, Debt & More." WealthyNickel. https://wealthynickel.com/personal-finance-statistics/.

Hill, Napoleon. *Think & Grow Rich.* New York: Chartwell Books, 2015.

Jacko, Dr. Joe. "Health Effects of Resentment and Forgiveness." LiveLongStayYoung.

https://livelongstayyoung.com/health-effects-of-resentment-and-forgiveness/.

Johnson, Robert A. *Owning Your Own Shadow: Understanding the Dark Side of the Psyche.* New York: HarperCollins, 1991.

Johnson, Sue. *Hold Me Tight: Seven Conversations for a Lifetime of Love.* 1st edition. New York: Little, Brown Spark, 2008.

Kabat-Zinn, Jon. *Wherever You Go, There You Are: Mindfulness Meditation in Everyday.* New York: Hachette Books, 2005. https://www.amazon.com/Wherever-You-There-Are-Mindfulness/dp/1401307787

Peck, M. Scott. *The Road Less Traveled: A New Psychology of Love, Traditional Values and Spiritual Growth.* New York: Simon & Schuster, 1978.

Rohr, Richard Rohr. *The Naked Now* (p. 170). The Crossroad Publishing Company. Kindle Edition.

Ruiz, Don Miguel. *The Four Agreements.* Amber-Allen Publishing, Incorporated, July 10, 2018.

Schweitzer, Kate. "Lawnmower Parents Are the New Helicopter Parents — Only They Might be Even Worse," Popsugar. August 9, 2019. https://www.popsugar.com/family/What-Lawnmower-Parenting-45235236.

Shahhosseini, Zohreh, Mehdi Pourasghar, Alireza Khalilian, and Fariba Salehi. "A Review of the Effects of Anxiety During Pregnancy on Children's Health," *Mater Sociomed.* 27, no. 3 (June 2015): 200–202. https://doi.org/10.5455/msm.2015.27.200-202.

Thorne, Blake. "Why Your Brain Has a Negativity Bias and How to Fix It," *I Done This* (blog). October 15, 2019. http://blog.idonethis.com/negativity-bias.

Williamson, Marianne. *A Return to Love: Reflections on the Principles of a Course in Miracles.* New York: HarperCollins, 1992.

Zuckerman, Arthur. "51 Gym Membership Statistics: 2020/2021 Data,

Trends & Predictions." May 20, 2020. https://comparecamp.com/gym-membership-statistics/

ENDNOTES

1. Kate Schweitzer, "Lawnmower Parents Are the New Helicopter Parents — Only They Might be Even Worse," Popsugar, August 9, 2019. https://www.popsugar.com/family/What-Lawnmower-Parenting-45235236.

2. Joe Contrera, *Extraordinary Results: Mastering the Art of Leading, Coaching & Influencing Others* (Prescott, AZ: Alive @ Work Publishing, 2018). The reader should consult Chapter 13: "Accountability, Pushback, & Curing the Dis-*Ease*."

3. Alan, Deutschman, *Change or Die: The Three Keys to Change at Work and in Life* (New York: Harper Business, 2007).

4. Marianne Williamson, *A Return to Love: Reflections on the Principles of a Course in Miracles* (New York: HarperCollins, 1992).

5. https://comparecamp.com/gym-membership-statistics/

6. Zohreh Shahhosseini et al. "A Review of the Effects of Anxiety During Pregnancy on Children's Health," *Mater Sociomed*. 27, no. 3 (June 2015), 200–202. https://doi.org/10.5455/msm.2015.27.200-202.

7. FTD By Design, "The 8 Different Types of Love + the Perfect Combo for You," https://www.ftd.com/blog/give/types-of-love.

8. Jon Kabat-Zinn, *Wherever You Go, There You Are: Mindfulness Meditation in Everyday* (New York: Ha-

chette Books, 2005), https://www.amazon.com/Wherever-You-There-Are-Mindfulness/dp/1401307787

9. Dr. Joe Jacko, "Health Effects of Resentment and Forgiveness," LiveLongStayYoung, https://livelongstayyoung.com/health-effects-of-resentment-and-forgiveness/

10. "Freedom," *Merriam-Webster Dictionary.* https://www.merriam-webster.com/dictionary/freedom

11. Andrew Herrig, "Personal Finance Statistics 2021: Shocking Facts on Money, Debt & More," WealthyNickel, https://wealthynickel.com/personal-finance-statistics/.

12. "Drug Use Statistics," Bedrock Recovery Center, https://bedrockrecoverycenter.com/drug-abuse-statistics/

13. Ashley Abramson, "Substance Use During the Pandemic," *America Psychological Association*, 52, no 2 (2021): 22. https://www.apa.org/monitor/2021/03/substance-use-pandemic#:~:text=Overdoses%20have%20also%20spiked%20since,those%20same%20months%20in%202019.

CPSIA information can be obtained
at www.ICGtesting.com
Printed in the USA
BVHW031519081222
653669BV00006B/15/J